'Of all Palmerston North's Creative Giants, poet and short fiction writer James Brown stands out for having written an ode to the city.' —Palmerston North Creative Giants

'These poems are political and personal and cryptic and funny and strange, and their freshness is guaranteed.' —Kate Camp, *NZ Listener*

'one of New Zealand's most adventurous and culturally savvy poets' —Mary Macpherson

'While James Brown delights in poetic constraints, and is dazzling within them, he can also blast away and, like the late night motorists on Fitzherbert Ave, has been known to throw beer cans and drop doughnuts, or their literary equivalent.' —Gregory O'Brien

'teeth and claws, social savvy, poetic sensibility, and stimulating peculiarities . . . a great reading experience.' —Elizabeth Knox, *NZ Listener*

'His goofy humour is quite contagious. Brown pens poems that are simple, restrained, yet border on something insane.' —Hamesh Wyatt, *Otago Daily Times*

'Brown is ever intent on disrupting the reader's expectations, on offering something unexpected.' —David Eggleton, *Sunday Star-Times*

'This is poetry that grabs hold of the world and gives it a shake.' — Hugh Roberts, *NZ Listener*

'His words get under your skin.' —Penelope Beider, *NZ Herald*

'The James Brown of New Zealand poetry.' —Dr Ernest M. Bluespire

'I like poets who let playfulness and humour be part of how they are serious: I mean poets like Jenny Bornholdt or James Brown or Hera Lindsay Bird.' —Bill Manhire, *Starling*

'Brown is bricoleur, a home handyman with found language; and unlike many of them, he puts it to proper use, makes poems with neatly mitred corners and doors that are hung straight.' —Anne French, *NZ Books*

'The poet attends in the warm auditorium, listening, sifting and making poems that shine from what he hears. The results are engaging, funny, sometimes maddening, and for all their anti-poetry interventions, oddly lyrical.' —Gabe Atkinson, *NZ Listener*

'His skill is apparent in moments of sly wit; a deft turn of phrase, an unpicking of theory, a very sure-footed word selection. It's like the snap of light off the tail of a fish as it about-turns under water.' —Sarah Wilson, *NZ Booksellers*

JAMES BROWN

Selected Poems

Victoria University of Wellington Press

VICTORIA UNIVERSITY OF
WELLINGTON
TE HERENGA WAKA

Victoria University of Wellington Press
PO Box 600 Wellington
New Zealand
vup.wgtn.ac.nz

A catalogue record is available at the National Library of New Zealand

ISBN 9781776563074

Printed in Singapore by Markono Print Media

Contents

from *Favourite Monsters*

from *Warm Auditorium*

from *Floods Another Chamber*

from *Go Round Power Please*

Responsibility

He listens to the birds toss notes
like pollen
through the warm fuzzy spring rain.
The garden is extrapolating
with unbearable bright green plastic.
It pushes through the walls,
noses convincingly over the floorboards.
He feels happy, lucky, nervous, stupid.
He is drowning in adjectives.
The air is palpable with unprotected sex.
She is a 70s woman
half in fashion
but just right now
she can't find the incense.

Creation

He loves her for her atmosphere.
Which is why it is so important
to mention the clouds:
what they are like, how
they seem slyly not to touch, but stand
freightless together, slanting to let in
select tunnels of light.
    But then that old boy outside
(the one about to come into view)
doesn't look so happy.
Standing there dripping
he looks like he knows how it feels
to be described as having
'come down with the last shower'.
Now the light breaks
across his shoulders like
pieces of some great glass elevator
he may have been waiting for
for years. Then the rain comes down
like glue. And on television
there is the Challenger,
not quite making it through
the hole in the ozone layer.
No wonder he turns away, that old boy,
the tunnel at the light's end
a mural on a brick wall.
    Though at the time it hardly mattered,
his sodden, leaden, darkened life:
because it seemed light-years away,
because it was hardly spoiling the view.
Because he was never supposed to be me.
Funny how you end up.
    But every story has two sides
(at least) was how I worked it
all those years ago. And
for the time being, I think that we
could let that one hold true.

For there is always an argument
to which weight can be lent.
Like, Jesus wants me
for a sunbeam, while
this is still my poem
where I am light in love.

Vanishing Point

It's a long way.
I have shaved off all my hair.
Breath 'obscures' the sky ahead.

You were rest assured and reading, but we
have not spoken much
since then.

Oh, by the way, we are in a car
travelling towards the someone
I hope will accept my proposal.

Here means ice-creams for dinner and
split decisions: both sides of the road
fading out and the cat's-eyes opening.

Distance brings its own relief.
The sky trails spilt milk.
You come to resemble your secrets.

You say you've been by this route before.
I hardly know.
And the snow failing.

You're the road by the river
with night coming on. Best press eject
and give me the tape.

Turning Brown and Torn in Two

You—a perfect reproduction
after a long day.
Smooth—folding through thin air
like a dart.

You lean against a wall
dropping leaves
or laughter—your eyes
lined with titles.

Is it not amazing
the way fingers filter down
—that tracing clipclip
of the runout groove.

It is barely an idea
how skin sails across the body
—a sheet of paper, warm
as a fresh photocopy.

Translation

The burnt-out bus sat waiting
by the empty houses.
A quiet time, mist gathered
in our mouths like broth.

We slit the blind boy's throat
and in his pockets found our hands.
I stole a smoky kiss, you pressing
worthless banknotes to my lips.

The wooden trees sucked dark birds
home to roost. We too kept to the woods
and there undressed, the last daylight seen
window-shopping in the topmost branches.

12XU

The jilted male is writing
a sorrowful poem
about his condition. Out
on the empty plain, under
the darkling moon, lost out
all along, in his room alone.

The poem is serious and sorrowful.
The male is listening to dark songs
about corners. He is listening
to his heart. His drawn, quartered,
repetitious heart. He feels
the words smitten in his blood.

It's raining. So here is the male
now walking home.
And he doesn't know
how, doesn't know how
to end, to end,
to end the rotten poem.

Betrayal

Easy to watch the words
as they slip out.
They could just be
popping round to a friend's
or taking out the rubbish.
Which, in a manner of speaking,
they are.
But once out, they're free,
free as you might only hope to be
—meeting, greeting, in a plunge-pool
of coincidental collisions.
Oh, the company they keep,
the combinations they assume
presume positions you would not
have thought physically possible.
Whereas you were never one
to raise your voice, your tongue
is raising questions, eyebrows, neck hairs,
in a tightening circle of suggestion.
For all the while
you have been lying
in bed, with your trembling lover
of many years. You had given
your word—so they say.
But now outside a voice
with your signature on it
declaims the most unspeakable
arrangement of terms.
And your silence lies there
hearing the screwed up letters
unfolding themselves in the rubbish bin
—the way your heart unfastens
and moves out through your chest
into the night sky.

Coming to Grief

Not so easy to stretch out a hand.
You are in the corner
getting smaller and smaller.

Outside the birds still sing
and the rain jams people in
the way it always has.

Soon now you will become a snail
curling into infinity.
Food is love, I say. Eat. Eat.

But you know food is not love,
and what or who should not be touched.
You feel   you know   too much.

And I am stretching out my hand
into the echo, into the
but   but   but   but . . .

Finally my heart splits.
That's the way with hearts,
they have a life of their own.

The day will always be cloudy.
The day will always be sunny.
The sadness opens out

and closes over.

I Do Not Know

after Jenny Holzer

I recognise
thin white bones
stretching into darkness.
Today I am finite.
I tick the box marked M.
To look within myself
I turn on the light.
I consume space
because it corners me.
When I call on my heart
it rings like an excuse.
Too much force
keeps me alive
but secretly I am
afraid of spiders.
I mark my offspring
but I wish they would
talk to me.
At work I employ people
to laugh at my jokes.
I would dearly love to
take you out.
I can easily ignore
the consequences
of what I implement.
Language organises
inequity.
I deliberately hold grudges:
they help me
meet the challenge.
Indecision collapses me.
If you question my methods
I shit in the woods.
Tonight I let you
change the channel

but I cannot be sure
if I still love you.
I take a drive.
Where I go is
none of your business.
Time is my dog
sometimes we play stick.
I know goal attainment
does not make me happy.
I know death
does not make me unhappy.
I wash off
reasonable doubt
in the shower.
Protect me from
what I want.
I do not know
if this is a poem.
I do not wish it
to be shared.

In Point of Fact

Your earth
is my inheritance.
I play the game
to the best of my
natural resources.
I want to go places
but Daddy is
no diplomat.
Public transport
swallows my pride.
All my friends
are called Dave.
I am always right.
Nirvana is
riding elevators
called Otis.
TV sets me up.
Each time I
sit around
I think I'm shot.
I am beautiful
and lazy
—which is fine.
Alcohol brings things
to life.
I tie people
to my feet
as shoes.
I saw this movie once.
What I hate
about Dave
is his give and take.
Meritocracy
created crime.
I imagine sex
to be like peaches.
I am always wrong.

I surprise myself
by not being hurt.
When I was young
I got the jug cord.
Everything bores me.
I masturbate
while thinking
about animals.
Good advice
is a treasonable act.
I lie with my lies
to find decisions.
My pressure is
in all the wrong places.
Help is not something
I cry for.
Appearances matter.
I am popular
with exceptions.
I am not impoverished
spoilt and happy.
Don't think I
didn't warn you.
I eat my dandruff.
I have that
petrol emotion.
My privilege
is a human right.
In point of fact
I just can't
ever ever ever
believe you.

I Think One Last

Not being too sure
I give myself
a good kick.
I buy things
that bring luck.
My broom handle
can be love.
The furniture is
full of secrets.
Naked men
make me giggle.
I admire my breasts
to see what might happen.
I wipe down surfaces.
For lunch
I eat my fingers.
The phone numbers
go down
like jellybeans.
My husband is
in and out
a good deal.
My mouth says
it likes sperm
—and it does.
Sometimes I make lists.
I must not mind
inhaling outside.
Pornography surprises me.
What I like about rain
is its gravity.
Electricity comes
from other planets.
You lick my lips.
I have learned
that sort of face
gets more time.

I just might.
I am important
and unnecessary.
What sparkle
I make up.
Then there are
many afternoons.
I spy
a Preludin sky.
It is inside
my experience.
It is nearly summer.
Here come
all directions.
I look at snapshots:
the father kneeling
by his lost sons.
I take a long time.
I will take a long time.
It will take a long time.
Every good boy
deserves fruit.
I think one last:
how disparate
from the world
is the text?
Once again:
how similar, how
unavoidable.

As It Happens

In which Juliet and Sylvia
make the acid drop in LA

Gradually mine eyes are jelly.
I go to the sideboard to get a
shriek-backed wrench. But
you win hands down by a head cold
of broccoli gone over. The bell jars:
a cage bringing us back to degree zero.
I smell a rat. Quickly,
the air is full of details, we
are out on the fire escape.
Oh the sweet city night when it is raining
and also when it is scorching.
We must clatter down and down
before the sight settles upon us.
Before the turbulent strips of characters
remove our clothing and
cover our bodies with oil.
I use the handles because they are
easier to grasp. Suddenly
you want to pee and now
you have done so. It is
an island in the blue linoleum
and we are flying down the corridor.
There is laughter and a good deal
of visual apparatus. I can smell
your spices. Sometimes
I can love the whole rotten world
when your effects waver towards me.
Then someone starts in on the
microwave jokes. So soon
we are short of breath
and have to go outside and be sick.
My eyes squelch the air
but again it is your trick
with a squat of warm, wet concrete.

A magazine woman gets out of the pool
and into her costume. I like
the way she looks at you, her
symptoms dancing like
Chinese water circles.
In the lantern light I
part my legs and watch
my fingers disappear.
As it happens her voice floats by
face down, a little above
the bottom of the pool.
You reflect on the glossy surface,
cinnamon lifting from your forearms.
The tiny blond hairs are moving
but no bubbles reach the air.
Far off there is lightning.
We do not stand on ceremony.
We each take a corner.
Everyone new is happy to see us.

Wiring the Present

You can tell me, I'm not listening.
The others are busy round the table
with the timer. The man with no soul
is giving directions. He looks almost imaginary.
He imagines our hands are tied.

The whole image looks almost imaginary
—I have had to invent the conversation.
Like I say, I should really have been listening.
I was trying to wrap the present
for our imaginary friend.

A glasshouse of roofing-staples.
I am surrounded by brown paper
and handfuls of bottlenecks. You can
feel my nails on the Sellotape,
trying to find the end.

The Temple of Lost Men

In the Temple of Lost Men
are many fine carvings and sculptures.
Clothing seems to have been optional.
On entering the Inner Sanctum
our pupils colour at the
full iris breasts and the
exaggerated manhoods.
Some of the statues
have eyes on their tongues.
It is not clear whether
these represent visionary speakers
or are warning us to watch what we say.
In the jungle many things are not clear.
Her drifting smile, for instance, and
who pulled the wings
from the beautiful song.

Cashpoint: A Pantoum

Welcome to Cashpoint
Open 7 days
Please insert your card
To begin transaction.

Open 7 days
Please ensure no other person can see
To begin transaction
Please enter your personal identification number.

Please ensure no other person can see
Select service required
Please enter your personal identification number
Use a blue key.

Select service required
Select from account
Use a blue key
Use a green key.

Select from account
Please enter amount required
Use a green key
Cash withdrawals must be in multiples of $10.

Please enter amount required
$10.00 entered
Cash withdrawals must be in multiples of $10
If correct press O.K.

$10.00 entered
If incorrect press correction
If correct press O.K.
Your request is being processed.

If incorrect press correction
Then press O.K.
Your request is being processed
Please wait.

Then press O.K.
Transaction accepted
Please wait
For further transactions.

Transaction accepted
Please remove card if you have finished
For further transactions
Select a blue key.

Please remove card if you have finished
Please remove cash and transaction record
Select a blue key
Thank you for using Cashpoint.

Please remove cash and transaction record
Cashpoint is open every day
Thank you for using Cashpoint
7 AM to 11 PM.

Cashpoint is open every day
Please insert your card
7 AM to 11 PM
Welcome to Cashpoint.

A Title

All this bloody poetry
plotting through
the pound and stash of sea

to grind up some grand and empty
God-forsaken beach.
(But not so soulless, God-withdrawn

to those lives and livings
there already. Their future
tense looms bracketed,

sporting ties and walk-on parts,
extras in a narrative
of somewhere else's art.)

Meanwhile . . .
the poem's tone continues lost
yet strong and searching

for the cadence
whose rise and fall seems
the swell of brooding green

—that burnt off and became
the rhyme of wind through pine.
Then narrow, modulated streets

nudged out through gorse;
homes packed in stanzas,
footy fields and power lines

leading to the corner store.
History/identity tied up
with Curnow's dog's pup.

It gnaws the poem
it is given to ignore.
And has nothing to do with me.

I live in the city.
That past—when the world
was black and white, like

old photographs or silent movies
on 'the telly' . . . some even claim
there used to be

just the one channel
there to navigate. Though
they can't recall its name.

Where are they coming from?
This poem doesn't need a title.
It knows who it is.

Diary Extracts from Scott's Voyage to Discover the West Pole

—'The sea is a woman who never grows old.'
　The crew sing to keep their spirits up.
　Yet song cannot silence our disappointment
　at being forestalled to the Pole by a bear.
　Although this Pooh is, of course, a stout English bear.

—The sea can never be judged too quickly.
　It is never as it appears / as it reappears.
　Gosh.

—We ate our last pony today—'Bolger'.
　I shot the brave little beast myself.
　Oh but he was lost and lame with no sea legs.

—Sun, salt, and more sun.
　How the green waves boil!
　How I long for ice and a cool breeze.

—I see the future as uncertain
　with my deteriorating humour.
　Yet our struggles are already immortal.
　Knock Knock we say.
　Amundsen who?

—Food is short.
　The tractors were not a good idea.

—This tropical heat does not agree with us.
　We have become argumentative.
　I am constantly having to cite the Concise Oxford.

—The most wondrous wave formations today!
　Like sastrugi. But in this humidity
　our photographic apparatus fails to function.

—We have lost Oates. We had gathered on deck
during a particularly bad bout of calenture.
He simply stepped over the rail to pick flowers.

—All hope is fading.
The sea is just there, it shines and shines.

—For God's sake look after our people.

The Poem that Took the Place of a Mountain

after Air New Zealand Flight TE901

Some New Zealanders
can remember
exactly where they were
that evening—like folks with
Elvis, Lennon, JFK—
while the flight crew
circled possibilities, until
the news eked out how
all available fuel must now be
or not—to—must now be.
    Of course the gas didn't actually
run out, till after
—purple over the ice.
It was time that ran out
—crept up like rising ground.
It was simply a sign—fuel—
one of many, one
we were all meant to
be or not to be
able to understand.
    It's a
particular tourist fear
—dislocation—though
we all like to know
where we are.
We like time and space
to negotiate
beautiful obstacles.
But beauty
is almost never truth.
Beauty is
beyond isobars, contours,
degrees, or definition . . .
waiting white as heaven's
perfect circle.

And then truth, you know,
that which you're persuaded
that you know, a given word
on which you're banking, curling,
weightlessly suspended
in belief.
     The great white silence.
A limit above compare. View
stretching like rumour
as far as the eye can see,
lying back, whispering
sweet nothings—an elaboration
hiding inside itself. Cameras
tilting at everything
not meaning to be there,
at anything becoming
a part, to all things
bright, insensible.
     Something starts whooping:
a representation of alarm.
The event horizon's
inclination to be
or not to be
now must be
now must have been.
     Terra, senses heightened,
rises to the equation
as time catches us all
staring, frozen;
minds blank when
the adjudicator
asks the question,
with six seconds left on the clock
to answer.

Metro

I

We tried roses
and found them guilty. We tried laughter
but were still sad. We went away somewhere

where we could be
really ourselves. The shelves
were full of crime and mysteries.

But there were also the long walks
and we took them—the sky
rushing up to meet us.

After dinner we sat back
chewing each other's fat,
trying to talk ourselves into

our own words. It was
a dark and stormy night,
full of straw people and masquerades

with their buckling freedoms of choice.
We made lists and waited. Life,
we wrote, is often listing.

II

Too much, too much,
cries the man in the next room
over and over.

Through the reduced options of a
speech impediment he recounts the war
as a time of clarity and focus.

'Keep your losses in the cross-hairs,'
his talk bubbles burble before him.
He would like them to take him away

but instead is offered home help and
a range of services, then left revolving
in the peeling wallpaper of his own voice.

III

You're falling. Every day of your life
you're falling, even though you may not
feel it—you may feel that you're

constantly arriving
in pre-planned situations, able
to get a handle on things and

pull yourself together. But you're falling,
over and over yourself, your fingers whistling
like rung holes through the smooth air.

IV

Good morning bathroom mirror.
You are not an oasis. Today you will not
buy the baby a new dress.

Who are the generous and what
are they saying? I am millions of people
facing millions of faces.

I water the goldfish.
In the stilted conversation
of breakfast cutlery, I was listening

to your eyes. The way they fell
like footfalls upon a fallen paper napkin.
Because at this point everything loses

purchase on the world—the butter knife
in its yellow brick, your dabbing gesture,
the waving of absent friends—there can be

nothing present but
the coming to and memory of
decisions. For that reason

always endeavour to claim preparation or
accuse luck. Move your arms as if marshalling
snap delusions of choice. Carry sheets of

A4 paper and request others write their
names and positions down upon them. Express
shock, but never surprise. Reward yourself: after all

V
it is important to be ready
to be lucky. It is important to get into perspective
the foregrounded generalisations

of the particular. This could be them now.
Her fingers twisting hand-holds in the eidetic
of a napkin, surrendered to the slip of air

and the sweet grief.
The slow-motion vowels of the goldfish
reversing like parachutes, back

up through the film of conversation
—already vapour and evaporating
to the horizon.

The necessary epidiascopic arrogance
of things which stand in for things
that can only negotiate their presence

through loan. So that in this world
nothing can be only itself,
and everything dead is buried alive.

VI

In a station, of the Metro
the sky rushed up
to meet us. As always

the bow-wave of air before
the volumes of hesitation. Then
there was the trick question

everyone always got right,
and the never-never ending
you could never work out

either.

from *Lemon*

(damaged by water)

For years I had read of the poetry
not (illegible) getting any
quite right. So (damaged by water)
if only I were better at sports.

The man on the park bench sat
(blot)ing his (deleted) smile.
The pigeons were very (crossed out).
The pigeons were very cross.

And then the (scribble) of your first
'commercially viable' single moves you to
(grey haze). It is still too sad and too long and
too like the Velvet (heat/light) in (unclear) places.

The (mildew?) comes in little puffy sniffs.
(smudged) the park bench, under the tall songs,
it's (indecipherable) how quickly
one's *pain au chocolat* is gone.

The Customer

A town with no windows.
Streets strewn with dead leaves
but not a single tree.

The girl who gave you your change
had a smile worth its salt, lips
the thin sheer of rind.
But it was the other one
you remembered.

Later, when you asked for her,
she no longer worked there,
they refused to know who you meant.

But you knew she would still be
waiting somewhere, in a dark room
down a darker corridor,
hand reaching quickly
inside the drawer, feet

cold as those stories
the match girl used to tell
before that long evening of snow.

A Theory of Relativity

Someone is padding softly through the room
next door, the knife drawer slowly opening . . .
You are starving, but there are many
worse off than you.

You are trapped in the middle
of a long, East European poem.
An old road alongside a field turns into
an old road alongside a field.

The jerrycan contains dirty petrol.
You could drink it, but instead
you pour it carefully over your head
before sitting down to wait.

Statement After the Fact

A woman was standing by the red barn.
There was a yellow dog
and a boy.

The sun was clouded
—but it wasn't gonna rain.
The sky was the colour of water
far off.

I didn't stop.
I had a good hat
and I
kept going.

Meditation 6

A is added to B.
A substitutes for B.
A is a superfluous addition to B.
A makes up for the absence of B.
A usurps the place of B.
A makes up for B's deficiency.
A corrupts the purity of B.
A is necessary so that B can be restored.
A is an accident alienating B from itself.
A is that without which B would be lost.
A is that through which B is lost.
A is a danger to B.
A is a remedy to B.
A's fallacious charm seduces one away from B.
A can never satisfy the desire for B.
A protects against direct encounter with B.

Notes

How flaky to decide
to compose you as music
when I can't even sing.
Or play an instrument.
That's why we have pop.
Here come your notable legs
—right on song.
All the leaves are *green*

From Today Personal Poetry Is Dead

Today the personal poem
wrote itself off.

The phone rang dry,
hung up to the
inevitable retention.

Effects stepped sideways
into space.

Time slowed
to an unsteady swing.

All about, the air tightened
with long sentences
falling short.

After a time-killing movie
—mid-afternoon—
the dark comes early.

Not even daylight is being saved.

Picnic at Darkness Falls

The man and the woman enter the frame
quite unexpectedly, he holding out his hand
to help her over the rocks.
It is late summer and the river isn't full,
but even so the black water
lives up to its name. Little buffs of foam
spiral outwards from the roar of the falls,
like stars or galaxies, or at least
those slow revolving swirls
in TV animations of the night sky.
Heavenly bodies as webs of filmy
plasma; how do we know
what distance really looks like?
The woman spreads a blanket
and together they lay out the food.
Then they smile and stare around,
momentarily awkward,
as if the act of getting settled
has used up all they have to say.
If some words pass between them,
you and I aren't able to make them out.
They both look uncomfortably happy.
And we want to preserve that.
We do. Because . . . because of the
soluble nature of happiness.
And comfort's dull recline.
We never abandon our dreams,
we siphon them off.
It is late summer, but at this angle
and altitude the temperatures
are more like early spring
—warm in the sun,
but otherwise leafy and microbial.
Nevertheless, the insect population
knows heat when it's on offer
and is a canvas of activity:
butterflies veer for the light,

a spider sets off across
the surface tension.
The man removes his clothes
and scrambles onto a rock and
prepares to dive. The woman
reaches for a camera, zooming in;
her frame, our frame,
the whiteness of his neck.
Relationships must take more attention
than we ever imagine.
A finger's gentle pressure.
Click.

Satellite

The baby in the womb
turns over and is lost
in red space—the last bee
in an abandoned honeycomb,
the last bee in trouble,
trying to find the exit
in the fire and the rubble.

The baby in the womb
stays quiet and unwritten
because its story
has already been told.
It motions secrets it cannot
possibly hold—the shades
between further
and farther—far beyond
its floating fingers.

Above and below
the temporary sky dawns
red and unready—its bloom
a folding bud. Today
the sunrise equals sunset.
It drains. It floods.
It turns its insides
inside out—the dawn rose
falling and falling.

Then it is still
for there is no more blood.
It is still
for there is no more water.
The mummy in the tomb
the baby in the moon
cold as tundra.

Redemption

The power's gone off, so I am taking
the opportunity to get something done.

> *Love is fires of Cellophane*
> *in a doll's house, in the rain.*

80% of life is just turning up
and already I am walking away.

> *The dark was talking to the dead;*
> *the lamp was dark beside the bed*

I will receive my redemption
and have no comment to make.

> *The missing room without a door;*
> *the footfall on the missing floor.*

Deliverance

after Bruce Weigl

Today, every day, this week, this year,
I have wanted to walk and keep walking.

I have wanted to slip, unaided, into water,
to let myself go of many things.

Such soaking rain this evening, Lord,
great full sobs, but warm—

the gutters overflowing like opened veins.
I lay down my arms and my cup runneth over;

all the futures I'd held in my hands
washed away.

Re: The Public

It's hard to know what 'the public'
really thinks.
Nine out of ten participants felt that 8.5%
wasn't 'nearly enough'.
We found this hard to explain;
were we asking the *right questions*?
Some people felt that, 'They all look the same, don't they?'
Some people felt that, 'Nobody likes a fuss.'
Were these the same people, *and in what ways*?
Were they the same people who said,
'Good folks, bad folks,
they generally look like what they are'?
Who said, 'I only know what I know'?
Were we asking the right questions *of ourselves*?
Some people ticked, 'At the end of the day, at the end of
the tether, at the end of imagining
there's always _____.'
They failed to understand, and were discounted.
Some people circled, 'So perhaps I'll see you tomorrow
my friend, my giddy roustabout, my little
ponga fence.'
They received full marks.
One person blamed 'the internal moon'.
One person wrote, 'Today we went to the wall and the pig.'
The majority indicated they only wished to be
'seated comfortably' when the balloon goes up.

The Acid House

Recently, a story I wrote called 'The Excursion'
was described by one reviewer as
'characteristically acerbic'. While I
(predictably) think that a slight
and (ahem) somewhat bitter reading,
it's the 'characteristically'
that really twists. Acid is only one of
many possible solutions.

In stanza two, I walk into town
to look for a job. There's plenty
needs musting, but no one's
willing to pay. The employed raise
their stakes and peer out, coolly.
In the dock, a boat called
The Spirit of Competition
looks like an upturned toadstool.

In stanza three, Anna (2) and I
are hiding behind the couch
with blankets over our heads.
We are waiting for someone to find us
and awaken 'a new re-birth of wonder'.
But the elegant passages are empty,
and we're couched within them, alone
and listening carefully . . .

Stanza four drifts in: grain silos,
the Cold War, an endless Midwest.
I mean, you learn and recite,
but always it comes down to
someone more powerful
one way or the other.
Sometimes the world is too much
to hope for.

New Zealand

after William Heyen

Custer and Crazy Horse meet unexpectedly
in their afterlives on the plain of eternal wanderings
—a prairie covered with spring flowers drifting
in and out of sunlight, like a bedspread set to airing.
The sensation is one of perpetual uplifting;
both Custer and Crazy Horse can sense this, know,
without knowing, the rising sky, the play of light,
the shimmering updraughts of landscape, and stand
before each other like painted backdrops.
'Hey,' says Custer, 'bygones be bygones,
it was a mistake, you know, the settlers,
the farms. It got out of hand, see.
I'm not saying you fellas were right, but,
Holy Mother of God, look at Los Angeles!
Let's shake . . .' He offers his hand—
But Crazy Horse remains in the pause,
as if waiting, his eyes—which continue
to remind Custer of messages sealed
in bottles—following the early morning mist
along the ridge   to where it precipices off
into thermals   and a hawk spiralling
until you might not be sure   whether it is
a hawk   or a piece of sky   or something
in your vision   and when you return
Crazy Horse is gone.

Identifying Zealand Birdsong

Listen: there's a tinted car hefting its way round Shipley Cres.
There's a ball bouncing onto the road.
There's a dog barking at someone out walking.
There's someone inside talking on the telephone.

The rates rise up, the rates rise down.
The new buyer is 'into sound'.
The bills arrive, the bills are paid.
The shopping's done, the table's laid.

There's a competition to be won.
All the unhappiness in the world.

Welfare

Having passed through the light
industrial zone, the flimsy houses
filed between vacant ground, the unleaded dogs
squirming within their lots, I present myself.

I present myself to you, suspicious behind your desk
in your cheap, serviceable clothes;
your cheap, serviceable clothes manufactured in the same
offshore sweatshops as my own.

'People are not here to serve the economy,' I say, 'the economy
is here to serve people.' One two three four five six seven eight
nine ten. 'Why was ten scared?' I say. One two three four five six.
'Because seven eight nine.' Because seven eight nine, ten.

I present myself to you on behalf of all those
who catch the shameful, mid-morning bus.
My black shoes stand on the floor.
My black feet stand in my shoes.

Paradise Regained

The future of our race will depend
on the internal combustion engine.
Everything will be drive-in.
Footpaths, parks, gardens, etc
will disappear, creating space for extra lanes
networking to wherever they're wanted.
Ground level will become
the domain of garages and intersections,
and we'll have cars to take us
to where our cruisers are parked.
Distance will be measured in traffic lights.
Of course, with 'increased efficiency', all that
carbon monoxide will still
kill us off. You try putting a tube
from your exhaust to your cab
and see how far you get.
Let's say, however, there are
a couple of people
whose lungs have mutated
so they can breathe carbon monoxide.
Maybe that guy in China
the Senator for Virginia saw smoking
two cigarettes at once—'That's the kind of customer
we need!'—and a woman cabbie from
New York—'It's fog, I'm telling ya!'
They will inherit the earth. We will be gone,
but they'll have the pick of the latest
twin cam, turbo-boosted, fuel-injected,
electro-luxury models—and
the super-highways to themselves!
In touch by powerful CBs,
they will speed toward each other
across the continent-connecting bridges
we were still paying for. No traffic jams,
no cops, no speed traps; just two dots
on the tarmac of the earth
—the genetic future of our race!

When they meet—somewhere on the
Aleutian Inter-continental—there will be
no customs, no immunity, no looking back.
They won't even have to worry about
where to park.

Discourse / Counter-Discourse

In the garden, the washing line
fell into disuse. First the women forgot
how to remove stains, then they
forgot cloth altogether.
They danced in celebration—
blood and chocolate everywhere.
Gradually, they forgot a lot of things
because there was no longer the anger
there to remind them.

Banished to the woods, the men
played patience and learned
to peg out their smalls.
There was much to be put right,
but they weren't worried.
At night they redrew
the pictures in the stars and
sure as eggs
knew they would be back.

A Bell Is a Cup

Imagine that, for this poem,
you have been transported to a beautiful,
uncharted island in the Pacific.

The island, which you can walk across in a day,
is teeming with birdsong and lush vegetation,
and also has its own supply of fresh water.

Imagine also that, as you're exploring,
you run into that special person you've
always dreamed of being able to get to know .

Perhaps they're your current partner, or a rock star,
or perhaps that shy but desperately attractive
person who sat opposite you one year in school.

Isn't it a shame how things don't seem to work out
like that? Though maybe in some poems they do.
Oh well, fuck. A bell is a cup, until it is struck.

Disempower Structures in the New World

A 2-litre bottle of Diet Coke
from the local dairy costs $3.50,
whereas a 2-litre bottle of Diet Coke
from the New World supermarket
round the corner costs $1.95.

A short walk therefore
through the new maths
appraises the situation, viz:

$$\begin{aligned} &\$3.50 \\ -\;&\$1.95 \\ =\;&\$1.55 \end{aligned}$$

where $1.55 approximates
net consumer loss, as well as
—on a different calculator—
potential retail profit.

You decide this knowledge is
'not cricket', but bottle it,
resolving—tomorrow—to visit
the New World supermarket
and then make the dairy owner an offer
of 2-litre bottles of Diet Coke
in a scenario rendered thus:

$$\begin{aligned} &\$2.65 &&\text{ergo} &&\$3.50 \\ -\;&\$1.95 &&&& -\;\$2.65 \\ =\;&\$.70c &&&& =\;\$.85c \end{aligned}$$

where 70c represents your portion
of the aforementioned
potential retail profit ($1.55)
—now redistributed
under new management.

If only you'd gone straight to the New World
—it also being open late every night,
thanks to the job-eager energies
of youth-rated young people, who will
still squeeze out smiles at 5 minutes to 10
and ask you if your day's going well.

Tonight, however, the dairy owner too
is (for once) unusually cheerful
as he accepts your money, chatting
about the cricket and asking
what it is you do.
'I'm in education,' you vaguely volunteer,
thinking of that final year for your BCA.
'Education—a good job, eh?' he says,
and asks about the pay.
'Mmm, 25 to 30 thousand,' is your dim reply.
'Yes, good job, good money,' he says,
'good money' shining in his eyes.

But now a child in pyjamas
is wailing, and he is talking
in another language, lifting her
onto the counter, while you are
hurrying home, checking
your change, counting
the silver stars in the night sky,
which are all lucky
and are all yours.

Waterford II

Recently, Tony O'Reilly—the Irish businessman
and sporting hero who owns Heinz and half the world's
newspapers—took over Waterford
crystal. He'd already passed up a career in
politics in favour of a wider market,
not wishing to be restricted to only the currency

of local taxpayers. Knowing the international currency
exchange (the exclusive realm of independent businessmen)
to be a truer site of power, O'Reilly set about investigating the market
for Waterford crystal—which is sold the world
over, but primarily in the US. In
the survey, US consumers of Waterford

crystal were simply asked whether they knew that Waterford
is in Ireland. If they did, the Irish workers held some currency:
since Waterford crystal had to come from Waterford, therein
lay their security against the strategies of global businessmen
and the ruthless mobility of capital around the world.
If, on the other hand, the US market

did not associate Waterford with Ireland, then market
forces could take over. Waterford's
crystal could just as easily come from somewhere else in the world,
like Poland, with the workers paid in their own worthless currency.
It's hardly poetry, but it made economic sense to the businessman's
brain of Tony O'Reilly. The answers which came back in

showed that very few US consumers in fact knew that Waterford is in
Ireland. Good news for the global market!
It would now be possible for Tony O'Reilly's business man
-agement team to negate the physical locality of Waterford,
taking only the history and the myth. The town no longer held
    currency
as a geographic location in the world.

In economic terms, it had become no more than a world
renowned brand name—an aura of quality captured in
crystal—that could be owned by anyone with the right currency.
It seems Foucault was right about power as a market
place. But what of Chomsky's Human Rights? In Waterford's
future, the dole queues snake while politicians offer tax breaks to
        entice businessmen.

But don't world prices drop as a result of international business man
-oeuvrings? Aren't cheap Third World labour costs passed on to eager
        First World consumers in places like, say, Waterford?
The faceless markets smile, as if to say, where does Chomsky think
        he's coming from, and, of what value today is a universal
        currency?

Acoustic Demos

xxxxxxxxxxxxxxxxxxxxxxxxxxxxxxxxxxxxxxxxx
I often ask myself, 'What's the good of poetry?'
I mean, for all that it wants to help—you can't eat it.
A voice then tells us how the acoustics in France
are (like everything else) the best in the world.
Listen, the voice keeps on in perfect pitch, listen
to the colours and the textures and the warmth—and, oh,
did I happen to mention the perfect pitch?

xxohxxxxxxxxxxxxxxxxxxxxxxxxxxxxxxxxxxxxx
Well, one day, we are playing pétanque
amid the ruined bookshelves of apartment blocks.
The balls go to ground—each hope a small fanfare.
At the same time, only later, their soggy reports return
like cannon-fodder from the surrounds
—or the music of hands clapping
to our ears—and are written down. Here.

There, in the notes of the songs attending the poem,
among the green fields and the soft summer breezes,
the red poppies—which are also to be found in France
(and are thus, also, the best in the world)—dance.
Hip Hip Hooray. Seventy-six trombones and a
Big Parade. Except nobody cheers, they just
stand and stare, and they turn their faces away.
xxxxxxxxxxxxxxxxxxxxxxxxxxxxxxxxxxxxxoh

After the Somme, Joe Christmas comes to farming:
belief and a wife above the Canterbury Plains.
*For we like sheep, for we like sheep, for weEEeeEEeeEE
like sheep*, again and again—his boy's relief fenced
in the woolly refrain. But the grandson finds
new flocks to watch: 5 o'clock shadow, 6 o'clock rock!
John/Paul vocals save his soul—it's a long way
to the shop if you wanna sausage roll.

xxxxxxohohohxxxxxxxxxxxxxxxxxxxxxxxx
We get into each other and turn on the CD.
This is the time, and this, the record of the time.
A bad system means lost reproduction
—it means long distance calls. The way credit
moves up and down the wavelengths,
the reverberation of applause . . . into
murderous surf upon far-flung shores.

xxxxxxxxxxxxxxxxxxxxxxxxxohxxxxxxx
xxxxxxxxxxxxxxxxxxxxxxxxxohxxxxxxx
We get out of the car and turn on the TV.
It's tomorrow's world today, where we're told that
there's a place for everyone on the field of play,
even the spectators—like the reader—may
invade the pitch. Although mostly they don't.
This is the civilised West.

While on Mars—which is neither here nor there—
the pitch of the course is, of course,
the question of First World oppression
through the exploitation and manipulation
of Third World resources.
Though she was just the cleaner, some nights
she danced me to the music of the ocarina.
xxxxxxxohxxxxxxxxohxxxxxxxxohxxxxxx

xxxxxxxxxxxxxxxhohoxxxxxxxxxxxxx
Yet because I play fair (but also for keeps)
lend me your ears and I'll give you the peace
of my mind with my choices of stance.
I scratch at my balls, tut-tutting nonchalant. Or I reach
for my snatch of privilege and catch myself nodding.
All those empty mouths—they should control their breeding.
oooooooooooooooooooooooooooooooooooooooooooooooo

73

oxhxoxhxoxhxoxhxoxhxoxhxoxhxoxhxoxhxoxh
We get over each other and turn on the remote.
We open the bottle and pour out its message.
The aquatic fields, picnics without clothes, the hills are alive
with the sound of mucus.
They say that once we all breathed water . . .
oxxxxxxxxxxxxxxxxxxxxxxxxxxxxxxxxxxxxxxxxh
I don't like the sound of it, unless it's art and I oughta.

No Trick Pony

The plain words—the best ones—
you couldn't give them away.

On the edge of the suburbs, it becomes hard
to come up with

other options—the skies so blue
you can hear yourself think.

More and more, closeness is required,
the collusion of cheek against stone.

Instead, the serene lawn mower,
who might be the both of us, circling into sleep.

Pond Life

I work all day
at my trade-offs.
Winning isn't
everything.
I reach out
to collect
my thoughts.
Dyslexics of the world
—Untie!
Is this all
I keep thinking.
Palmerston North
—Knowledge City.
Desire is
where people
don't live.
A bird in the hand
is worth
less than it was.
Let us
walk over the lake.
I respect
your positions.
Vacancy.
Together we
undress the balance.
In case of fire:
keep quiet.
Your options are
always open.
Hamilton
—where it's happening.
SOH
essential.
Let us talk
over each other.
I am not

a bicycle.
Your space
fills my time.
Don't mind if
I do.
I'm sorry?
What is it
you're reading?
Congratulations!
Dunedin
—it's <u>all</u> right here.
You hear
what I am
saying.
My
critical mass
gathers no moss.
I have nothing
to give
to society.
People
are jealous.

A Serious Assault on the Senses

The road to glory is uphill
and paved by rain.
A man on a corner stands arguing
with a man in a doorway
about a car.
One of them picks up a rock.
This is a shit neighbourhood,
you can't even pick up a woman.
A briefcase on a back seat:
still life with bullet points.
Behind glass, the unique woman
waves farewell to the icy trawler.
Some marbles belonging to
The Order of Disclosure
stray onto the footpath.
A mysterious blind person is seen
leaving the forecourt of the service station.
One of the men is capable of being
so besotted by anger that his head
becomes a mug shot, his thoughts
a bushfire at sea.
The Pajero with briefcase
roars past in a cloud of opera.
A serious assault takes place.
The unique woman is divided.
The other man shrugs his palms
in the gesture of someone
who has no memory and no
information.
The expanding background
tears along the hairy causeway.
I wish I'd done sciences.

The Language of the Future

for Catherine

In the language of the future
today will always be today
and the moments will sparkle like bearings.
There will always be enough time
to get things done
because there will always be
enough hours in the day.
Countries will be divided up
into hexagons, and every hexagon
will be occupied by
a new idea. Everywhere
will be connected directly
with everywhere else
by the infallible laws
of perspective.
Straight lines will flow
into straight lines
across the golden fields,
across the golden fields melting
into the golden cities.
Gold will grow on vines.
In the future, language will also
grow on a vine, and everything we say
will be understood. People
will be able to speak their minds,
so that the world will seem
at first astonishing
and then strangely quiet. Some will begin
to choose their words carefully, but most
will come to regard communication
with a lengthening suspicion, so that eventually
the sounds themselves
will be granted independence
—and then held accountable.
As such, in the language of the future
the revelations of the new freedoms

will be the property of everyone
and nobody.
Breasts will become a
universal validating standard
and fat people
will be made illegal. Cars
will finally be included in
the Bill of Rights
and granted protection from
pedestrians
and other forms of
visual pollution.
The emancipation of signs
will be the speed of change.
For in the future, brain retention will decrease
but thought-count will expand,
so that poking out one's tongue
will be just the tip
of the iceberg.
And although the space separating words
from everything else
will have ceased to be, research will continue
and a distant descendent of Henry James
will discover a way of measuring exactly
the spaces *between* words.
Mapping will begin, and the first settlers
will arrive and gaze straight through
all that lies before them
into
whatever will be.
With the new discoveries
the insides of language
will be found to be made up of
trillions of interconnecting spheres.
Thus, the insides of many things
will come to be similarly
constructed, so that when a man
inserts his opinion
into a woman, her insides too

will glisten with spheres, which will whirr
and retract and increase slightly
in temperature. Teenagers courting in parents' cars
will no longer do donuts, but will do spheres,
and, as the verbs decline, their rear-vision mirrors
will display the past
like kinetic sculpture.
Babies will start to be born with wheels
making it easier
to get around.
Within the language of the future
everything will be different
and instantly recognisable.
We will touch our golden bodies together
and they will touch their golden bodies
together, and so on and so on.
But there will still be the stories
for we will always have the need
to be guided by voices. 'Listen,' they already whisper,
'under the bushes, under the stars,
a cool hand talks silently, love . . .'

from *Favourite Monsters*

The Day I Stopped Writing Poetry

The day I stopped writing poetry
I felt strangely serene.
Back when I first started, I had no idea
what I was trying to do: get something out, perhaps,
and I suppose 'art' had something
to do with it. There's a tempting simplicity
about poetry; you don't necessarily need
the room, the desk, the glowing typewriter
—a scrap of paper and a pencil will suffice.
Some of my tidier lines often came to me
on the bus or while I was just lumping along;
they'd be dancing or singing away in my head
while I grinned helplessly at the passing world
until I could arrange to meet them somewhere.
But of course the passing world passes by,
and poetry isn't prose, or Java, and in the end
the time/money equations just don't add up.
Poetry's biggest strength is also its biggest weakness.
Remember I said how poetry doesn't need
the desk, the 2000-words-before-breakfast, etc?
Well, I lied (something else poetry's good at).
More often than not it does, and you find yourself locked
in the doll's house of your skull for days, months, years even,
trying to find a way out.
Sometimes you do, sometimes you don't—that's by the by—
the point is you haven't finished a novel
or a short story, or got anywhere near Java,
and there are bills to pay, children to feed, etc.
So the day I stopped writing poetry
I felt strangely serene.
3:44am, Wednesday, November the 3rd, 1999.
That was it—finished.

The Cost of Living

Isn't it amazing, the Old Masters tell us,
how after someone's death, or birth,
or something equally momentous, the world
'sails calmly on' or 'the small drops
stream down panes of glass . . .
gathering,
as they always have,
in pools on the ground'.

It was like that the week of your death
as I walked through the spring air
to the supermarket:
the rain swung about;
birds chirped in the school playground's
felled tree; the cars ignored
the zebra crossing.

And in the supermarket
everything was in its place. Oh sure,
some items were on special, others not, and new lines appeared
to sell the old lines in different ways. But Wilson Pickett
was still waiting for the midnight hour at four in the afternoon
with the same level of anticipation
he would still be waiting for it with
at four the following afternoon.

One door closes, another door opens, I thought
as I left. Everything is as it should be.
Then on the radio at home I learnt how
the price of groceries had risen over the June quarter
and that, even though offset by other factors,
the cost of living had quietly and imperceptibly
gone up.

Loneliness

I was just sitting there, wandering lonely as a cloud, when
—honest to heaven—looking out of the window
I saw Elvis. I know I know, but honest to heaven
it was him—or my name's not James Brown.
There he was, just walking across the quad in no particular hurry,

briefcase under one arm, an airy spring to his gait,
his five-inch DA glistening in the breeze.
But right off you could tell he was going places;
he didn't look left or right, just ahead where he was walking.
Mid-period Elvis. His leather jacket passed within five feet of me.

And I wasn't alone, plenty of students saw him too. An older one
—probably a third year—went up and shook him by the hand.
Young women clustered in groups, glancing and whispering.
A couple of likely lads snapped their fingers. There was a palpable
happiness, for once you've seen Elvis you are never alone.

He was whistling softly. Not a curl, more an expression
of frankness was pursed on his lips as he passed (I noticed
the first signs of comfort eating just starting to grace his jowls).
I couldn't quite make out the tune, but now I hear it as
the fadeout to '(Sittin' on) The Dock of the Bay' by Otis Redding.

It was autumn, the odd lost leaf left dallying in his wake
as he turned the corner by the silver birch trees.

The Batcave Show

I once did a late-night radio show on the local student station.
From the first I used a pseudonym—not that anyone
would have believed me if I'd used my real name.
I also had a part-time job in a record shop, and one day,
while I was working, I struck up a conversation with a listener
who had no idea I was the late-night announcer.
For some reason I found myself criticising my show
to see how the listener would react.
He was very sincere, and no matter how gently
I tried to suggest that the late-night announcer tended to
'go on a bit' or was 'too opinionated',
he never joined in my bad-mouthing.
But he was such a nice chap
that he didn't want to argue either,
so he just said 'Mmmm' a lot.
I remember being particularly interested to know
what he thought of the music I played,
so I would lead in with 'The music's OK, but
don't you think it's sometimes a bit . . . wanky?' Or 'commercial?'
Or 'obscure?' I gave him every opportunity to let fly,
but he would just say, 'Mmmm, sometimes. But not always.'
Now, I can vouchsafe that he didn't know who I was
because some months later we ran into each other again
and I fessed up and we had a good laugh about it.
To tell you the truth, I was a bit embarrassed
—him being such a nice chap—
and I did my best to explain how my motives
had been based purely on market research
and that I hadn't just been trying to pull his leg
out of its socket.
At that time my radio show was, to a large extent,
a reflection of my personality, or at least the personality
I would've liked to have had, and I desperately wanted it
to appeal to certain sorts of listeners. And, apart from being male,
my listener was exactly the sort of fan I wanted tuning in.
Which he continued to do: sometimes he would ring me up
and request songs and, every so often,

he'd tell me how he'd once met this person claiming to be me,
and that I'd better take care,
because you could never be sure what was going on
inside these people's heads. You could never be sure
what was going on
inside anyone's head.

The Truth About Love

She left and I had a balloon in my stomach.
I am not much given to conversation
so I went out for a walk, which is sometimes
a good way of clearing the air.
I didn't know where I was going;
I drifted in and out of jobs, in and out of favour
with several disappointed women.
Then at the corner of One and T'other Streets
I came across a slow-moving queue,
which I joined: we all need to belong somewhere.
When I finally reached the front,
a funambulist directed me to a further queue.
I could not see exactly how long this one was
because it disappeared over a cliff.
Aha, I thought, now at least we're getting somewhere.
On reaching the edge, I saw that the cliff was, in fact, very high,
but things seemed to be moving quickly now.
On the bloodied rocks below sat a mermaid
with long blonde hair and peeping breasts.
She looked up and waved to indicate
she was ready for me.
But I had forgotten about the balloon and,
as I stepped out, I bobbled away.

Alt. Country

for Fergus

I left the university and my mind
lit out for the territory; it was time
for a real job, time to
get my hands dirty and make some
real money.
I shouldered my guitar and kissed
the favoured members of my family
Goodbye.
Did I embrace my loved one
with a rough tenderness
or did I embrace *only the moment* . . . ?
Wild skies.
I grunted farewells to friends,
but friends' friends met with my
honest indifference.
Those who thought themselves special tried
talking me round: did they
write their scripts in the shower?
There was, however, the 'girl with promise' to consider,
and I did, incrementally, though eventually
settled for just a curt nod in her
general direction. Ha! Where I was heading,
acquaintances would be no different
to the one-hitch towns
through which I would regularly be passing.
People as places, places as people—yes
that was the way to play it. No more grief.
By the time I got home, I was feeling better.
I was through with being cool,
and ready for dinner.

The Pursuit of Happiness

A sadness descended over me
like the grey blanket of mist
that crept in from the sea
over Baskerville Marsh

until I couldn't see my hand
in front of my face. Only
the hapless squelch of my
shoes was loud to my

ears, and the distant baying
of the hound, ever closer,
as I blundered on, praying
for him to find me.

Guilty Spaces

There are a lot of things going down
in the world right now—both good and bad—
but not a lot going down down here, Lord,
sure as I am sitting here writing this
and sure as you are sitting up there reading it
(as I know you to be doing).
But that is not to say
that a lot of things haven't happened, Lord,
that all the easy times have been nice quiet drunks,
or that a lot of things don't continue to happen,
sometimes at the stroke of a pen, oh God,
or that a lot of things won't go right on a-happening
out there beyond what it is our understanding to know.
What I am saying, Chief—with respect that you've maybe
had yourself cause to glance in my direction before—is that
this time I am truly fully sorry for all the trouble
I know I have maybe caused.
I know it's no blame use trying to take things back,
but working hard like I done most all my life
never seems to have helped me any, and those times
sitting round idling with Old Hob ain't ended up
no Christmas neither. So what I am saying, Lord, is that
I now know I need your help to get the black Jack
out my hand for once and for all. I need you
to show me the way of acsension into your house.
It ain't no use me gambling on myself.
This time I have taken the decision for real.
Lord, I just need your forgiveness and guidance
and the bounty of your ever-loving hand
to ensure safe passage. $5 oughta do it.

Good Books

Poetry doesn't give enough
information. People don't like it
because they don't like absence.

Blanks remind them
of exams, of death
and the void.

That's why in the beginning
was the word
and the word was God.

And the more words gather together,
the more options. People like
to shop around.

Take the good book:
God went right across the page,
though in crucial respects

never made it
to the end of the line.
But the balance was right,

He was on to a winner.
My advice? Stick with prose
and spread your investments.

There's safety in numbers.

Snapshot

The day orange. He gazed out over the area.
He surveyed the area. Angles, distances
he already knew. A slight breeze,
which he would leave to instinct.

The woman came up behind him and touched
his shoulder. He could smell her excitement;
her excitement smelled like boiled clams.
He thought of his mother, her voice pinking down the thread

of her worsted life, his father marching out of the room.
He knelt down. He could see the first glints of the motorcade
down the long, tree-lined avenue, coming toward him
like the future.

Out of Eden

They tandemed,
she talking all the miles.
Something could be done with this terrain,
he thought, but I'm not sure what.

It was stinking hot. Again.
Women, she explained, get a raw deal:
chafing, period pain—men.
A stick caught in their chain.

They both needed to go,
so they stopped.
He turned against a tree and peed his name.
She was careful not to wet her socks.

They started up again:
two circles, joined
and separated
by a frame.

Other Ideas

So there we all were at last. All three of us.
We were mature, talked hard and long into the night,
as if the words would somehow cause less fuss.
If this is wrong, then maybe this is right,

we reasoned, but . . . what a load of shite.
In the morning it was me who caught the bus.
You came down to see me off, your night
face still lovely in your morning hair, unbrushed.

The Pleasure Principle

We gazed into each other with flat-out gravity.
There was no room for lightness in the dark's chowder.
You could say we were bound together by our mutual taste.
You could say we were a pair of hands rubbed in avarice,
a giant spider oozing out a thread.

But there was no thinking about the ins and outs.
There was no thinking.
Pleasure must be worked open like a birth,
pressed out like wheat until a splayed husk,
until it is flour and the rain comes.

Family Planning

I came back into the afternoon,
but you weren't happy to see me.
You were tangled in circumferences:
the children ran around like snakes.
'Impossible,' I said, 'this whole situation.
You no longer peel me out of my wet day
and dry me off with your tongue
the way you used to of an afternoon.'
Your eyes were puffballs; your compact body
—between whose symmetries I'd played so happily—
another life. Your hands searched each other
for grains of rice. To fill the silence
I thought of your deflated stomach
swollen in the act of childbirth, your arse
arching like a baboon's.
'Forgive me,' I cried, 'I was lying.
Out there everything is a lie.
Situations get lost in transition.
The children are so beautiful.
They are almost treacle.
After dinners, baths and impossible stories,
let us abandon them to the raft of sleep
—give it a really good shove—and meet
somewhere—an island of shocked blossom—
a contradiction bigger than haiku anthologies—
where we can gather or steel ourselves
—whatever has to be done—
for the sake of the future.'
You puffed a cocked eye and moved your lips
across mine like a kind word.
'Are you suggesting we should
have another child?' you said.

Maintaining the Family Unit

Desire creates a context,
    after that it's just details.
I look for a handy height on which to lower
    your gleaming underside.
Likewise, this sort of poem is easy to do
    badly.

Outside, a tennis match sweats it out
    —agh/thwack, agh/thwack—
and I think of tennis balls:
    their squishy muscle tone,
        their fine layer of down,
            their good handful.

Adaptability is the salient feature
    of the family unit.
The unit is usually located in the kitchen,
    but often functions best when
its state-of-the-art components are asleep in their rooms
    and the two main constituents
are connected up
    on top of the dresser.

Feeding the Ducks

We are all all right. Dirty and bedraggled,
but all right. Tessa (1½) sits in the pushchair
leaking river water and mewing softly to herself.
We unravel her clothes until she is
a chattering pool on the back step,
a tadpole to be carried to the bath.
You comb the river bottom from her hair,
while I trawl her tiny silted layers in a bucket.
I add my jersey with its wet hug-print down the front.
The fire will not light. Anna remembers the ducks
laughing.

Mist Conception

The mind gathers in emptiness.

Snow beneath trees.

Trees beneath snow.

The blank pages turning to each other.

Capitalism Explained

A guy at school once
told me how he'd buy winegums
for 2 cents each and

sell them to his
little sister, who wasn't allowed
out to the dairy,

for 4 cents each.
If it was raining—5 cents.
That about covers it, he said.

Forgiveness

The white man is good at impersonations.
See him act the goat.
You laugh along—you're both
away laughing.

Then—snap—his smile is gone.
You've said something wrong,
something critical
that has lodged

a heart in the matter.
The white man's mouth settles
for a hard line.
You don't know where you stand.

You open your hands,
but the white man
isn't giving anything
away.

The White Girl

She was all shy, the white girl,
and sweet as pie.
And a type of clever, with more letters
than her name—

lined up, ticked off, like places
passed through on a train.
Either she was genuinely bright
or, like most accomplishment,

the endpoint of good training,
luck and knowing
how to play the game.
Whatever, butter wouldn't stain . . .

She married well. Wrote a novel.
Yet always the little smile,
the earnest brow, an insider voice
whispering sell, sell now.

Hard to tell. Hard to tell.

All We Have

after Jenny Holzer

Memories are
always precious.
It's unhealthy to be
too much yourself.
Love is worth
every penny.
You can only rely
on your enemies.
The old ways
will come back.
Hope is
a glass slipper.
Tough backgrounds
should be considered.
Talent and daring
win through in the end.
Honesty is
the best fallacy.
The well-off
deserve a break.
Religion gets
too much blame.
Children are
a necessary evil.
Polygamy is
the way of the future.
Good days
are just a blur.
Wisdom knows
when to play dead.
Beneficiaries need
a kick up the jacksy.
Guilt can never be
forgiven.
Being hungry is
no excuse.

Penny Wise
gets what she deserves.
The arms race is
there for the taking.
Errors of judgement
happen to everyone.
A helping hand
walks under ladders.
Repetition is
a big yawn.
Being true to yourself
is just stupid.
A big smile
surprises everyone.
It's best not to say
what you think.
Success is mostly
dumb luck.
Presentation means
more than content.
Nostalgia is
not what it was.
At the end of the day
the sun sets.
We've got to believe
it's getting better.
Generalisations are
all we have.

Engagement

Everybody in the world is engaged
in some sort of pursuit, probably.
I pushed us off and we were away:
wooden crates overflowing with apples,
goldfish in plastic bags, all of us
bobbing slowly through the generations.
Ah, the perfume of the past
and its uncontrollable distinctions:
mango chutney over chicken
and then everything but
the kitchen sink overflowing with rimy dishes.
Oh the abomination of desolation!
Some seeds fell by the wayside.
She had coal dust all over her skirt.
Nothing is ever the way they say it is.
By my God have I leaped over a wall.

Born Sandy Devotional

She lay down by the river.
Her hair trailed, found its own level.
The light was soothing, classical:
piccolos of rain fell softly.

Give us this day our daily . . .
and so on.
When I began, I didn't know
right from wrong,

what from what.
It was hot.
Swallows flipped out
over the mudflats.

She was born sandy devotional.
The emotional landscape
is always and only ever made up
of sand.

We loosed her threads—remember?—you
kneeling out back of her
gulf's
wide swing tremolo.

Soup from a Stone

He rejoiced at
the dazed white doves

that found their ways
to his balcony,

bedraggled and stone-deaf,
and gave thanks to

Frau Hinter,
his bird-loving neighbour,

and to the butterfly bomb
which had flown

into the coop and
opened its ribcage.

He would coax each
refugee from its perch;

the trail of crumbs into
his darkened sanctuary

becoming the onyx stations
on a paperweight

he'd uplifted
from a gutted church

in southern Italy
and with which

he'd anoint
each small bent head

before plucking and curing
for his pot.

It was 1945 and the ears
had walls. He'd heard

it would end soon, but
had swallowed enough

baloney in Italy.
His wife and child

were dead
and he was fed up

and hungry.

The Radiant Fuel

In the upper atmosphere above the dusty settlement
the humidity is nadir. No rain today.
No rain for the last five years. The eternal combustion engine
parches out the layers. There is nothing to eat.
You must be careful
where you place your feet.

While shepherds watch their flocks,
a goat stamps a cloven hoof and blows sky-high:
a rain of blood and meat. The tenth, and least important, child
is dispatched to gather tea. The fire requires fuel.
Two one-legged men propel
a single bicycle downhill.

It is cool in the pool
at the secret desert location—until the red phone rings.
More trouble. Well who in hell was stupid enough
to book a Holiday Inn?
Don't bug me with heavy metal or malaria.
Secure the area.

It is cool in the shadow of the holy miracle.
There are no complaints about sanitation.
The women prepare dinner.
The guards change when the muezzin calls to prayer.
The leader tells us what is in the air. A mullah crouches
with a video camera.

There is no defence. You cannot
build a fence. Gorged on our country's riches as you are
our martyrs will walk in and out your mouth
like flies on a dead man.
Your country will unfurl
the most advanced graveyard in the world.

Puff adders in the bran tub;
the smile of terror brings a thousand eyes.
The sent men come again; they take
my children and they share my wife.
They say to go with them. They say
the time has come.

People. People and dogs. A man
with a turban like a porkpie hat. A child wailing
by a wall. Soldiers prod a woman at a tap.
Take that. A small hand draws
upon a stone. A nearby man
is setting up a stall.

Still only fire from the sky. The ground
burns underfoot. Children perch on APCs.
They have no arms, and so they wave.
They have no cup, and so their hands make ripples.
They have no choice, and so they are
the chosen.

Instructions for Poetry Readings

1. The Poet

Seem a little arty and off-beam. It's important
to look like the sort of person that poetry
might happen to. Model yourself
on previously successful poets, who have,
after all, set the standards in this area.

In the live setting personality is, in all honesty,
probably more important than your poetry.
It's necessary to find a happy balance between shyness,
which the audience will equate with humility and
sensitivity, and slick patter, which the audience
will equate with wisdom and authority.
Be humble, you have been invited to read
(you were invited, weren't you?),
but be at ease with yourself in front of the audience
for you are in the spotlight and nobody wants
to see you mumble and burst into tears
any more than they want to see you
play air guitar and pitch face first
into the drinks table.

If you haven't been introduced (bad organisational form),
say who you are and where you come from.

Read from your book, or read poems you've had published,
because that's what the audience will have to do
if they ever want to encounter your work again.
I suppose the point here is that though your latest poem
might be the most riveting thing for you,
the two people in the audience who have heard of you
probably want to hear something they know.
But don't do a big ad for your book or poem—it's uncool;
if people are really interested they'll hunt things out.

Also, when I say read from your book I mean
read from something, even if you know your poems
off by heart. Blank sheets of paper are fine.

This is to do with appropriate eye contact.
Nobody wants to be eyeballed by a poet in full flight.
The audience has come to stare at you, so let them. Perhaps
glance up now and then to make brief, kind-eyed contact
with certain people and the disinterested middle-distance
—which is where most of your poems are going anyway.

Should you tell little stories about your poems before reading them?
An emphatic Yes! People find poetry difficult enough as it is
and this may be the first and last time
the audience ever encounters your work.
So don't worry about directing them, they need it.
Stories also give you the opportunity to reveal your personality,
which, as previously mentioned, is probably more important
than the poems anyway. And people
are also likely to enjoy the stories more too.

Don't go on too long. If the story becomes longer than
the poem, you've probably got the balance wrong.
Long-windedness is a sign of being too comfortable
in the limelight and tips the personality scales towards
unbecoming showiness. Poetry is about brevity
and choosing your words carefully:
it's better to read for less than your allotted time
than to seem like a frustrated novelist.

Don't read too fast. Don't worry about your weedy voice.
Pause. Take good breaths. Emphasise. Follow the cadences, line breaks
and rhythmic variations. Pause again. Have a drink of water.
If you can do different voices, do—this is a performance.
Some gesturing may be permissible, swaying is fine,
but nervous fidgeting or dancing around and striking poses
can distract from the words, which are, in the end,
the principal performers—right?
Go for it. Speak your poems clearly in the way
you intended them to sound.
This is their best chance.

A word about mics. Adjust the height before you begin;
your mouth should be about two fist lengths away.
It's sometimes a good idea to ask if everyone can hear.
Turn slightly to the side whenever you come to a P,
otherwise you'll be 'popping your Ps', as it's known.
Sibilance and feedback are the soundperson's fault.

Smile. Thank everyone for listening and (maybe) the organisers.

2. The Audience

Arrive in good time: coming in late to a poetry reading
is like bursting into applause at the end of the first dramatic
pause—only the other way round. Also,
the poet is panicking that no one will turn up,
so being early is a special act of kindness in that sense too.
Leaving early is maybe worse than being late, so if you do
suffer from ADD, crabs or incontinence, sit near the back.
Otherwise, sit near the front: poetry readings are usually
intimate affairs and no one likes to visualise an intimate affair
as row upon row of empty seats.
Grin like you've been looking forward to it for weeks
—see, even the audience has a vital role to play
in the performance. You may need to practise.

Children really shouldn't attend.
Firstly, it's not fair on the child, and, secondly,
they lower the strived-for artistic pretence.
The occasion is, after all, a poetry reading
not a folk jamboree. Controlled dogs, however,
are perfectly acceptable.

Talking or whispering during the reading
is strictly forbidden, even if
you are the only audience member.

Between-poem interjections push the boundaries of etiquette,
but certainly jolly things along a bit
and are a way of immortalising yourself.
The reading may forever be remembered for
'that big lady' who called out that she too
'used to live in Sanson'.

Negative responses are more tricky than might be supposed
because, remember, the poet is in 'performance mode'
and may well be highly articulate
as to the merits or otherwise of certain poems or procedures.
It's also worth noting that most of the audience
are likely to be at least sympathetic to the poet
and you could well find that there is
'more than one Poozer in Pompelmoose Pass'—as it were.
If you have really disliked a reading,
the standard procedure is to take a trusted friend
to a café afterwards from where you can safely
flay the poet's reputation beyond an inch of its life.
Check that they aren't sitting behind you first.

Clapping is ordinarily reserved until the end
of a poet's 'turn', but outbursts of appreciation
after a particularly memorable poem
are not unheard of.

Other nonverbal appreciations are acceptable
and may even be uttered while a poem is still being recited.
Clicks, tuts, mmms and chuckles are common.

Throwing money has, to my knowledge,
never been attempted, but poets are usually open
to new experiences.

Sleeping is acceptable, but snoring and/or
falling from one's chair are considered
bad form.

Sleeping with the poet: because this is best
not attempted until after the reading has concluded,
it falls outside the jurisdiction of this poem,
save to say that it is a very murky area,
one within which all parties are likely to end up
getting what they deserve.

Buying the poet's book and getting them to sign it
will make you a friend for life. Do you really want this?
Unless you get particularly carried away by your role
in the 'performance' aspect of the event,
it's best only to buy a book for genuine reasons because:
1. there's no sense in encouraging someone whose work
you don't really like, and
2. favours aren't always returned.

A final word. Expect nothing and you won't be disappointed.
Above all, at least try to look as though you're paying attention.
That way nobody gets hurt.

from *The Year of the Bicycle*

The Bicycle

I have always been lucky.
When I was seven
my parents gave me
a red bicycle.

I rode it every day until
it became a part of me.

It had a basket on the front
and my father attached a bell
to make doing the deliveries
more noticeable.

Pedalling up hills
pushed me so far inside my head
that only reaching the top
could bring me back out.

Going down, my mouth would open
as the world became flocks
of many-coloured birds
soaring into flight.

I loved that bicycle.

Lying in bed listening
to rain sheet against the window
and knowing that tomorrow
it was Monday,

I would get up and go
into the hall and stare at it,
consoled by the standing
of its beautiful silence.

I Come from Palmerston North

The fact of the matter is
I was born at Palmerston North Public Hospital
at 12:40am on the first of April, 1966.

My father, Timothy John Brown, tried to get the date
put back to March 31st
in order to claim a full year's tax rebate
from the government.

The following year the Beatles released *Sgt. Pepper's*
and the Velvet Underground released *The Velvet Underground and Nico*.
My initials—JSB—are the same as Johann Sebastian Bach's.

My father and mother are not originally from Palmerston North.
They immigrated there from across the world and never left,
even though they managed to leave each other.

The Palmerston North Boys' High School yearbook is called
The Palmerstonian. But I do not think of myself as a Palmerstonian.
People from Gore do not think of themselves as Gorons.
I come from Palmerston North.

While still attending PNBHS, schoolboy Craig Wickes played
14 minutes for the All Blacks against Fiji in 1980. Imagine
the town's pride and anxiety as, ball in hand,
he ran at his opposite number and bounced
out of contention.

He once threw mud at my friend Robert Rieger.
Robert is the son of Paul Rieger—a long-time Mayor of
Palmerston North. Robert also went on to become very successful
—as a Catholic priest.

1994 was the year Palmerston North changed its subtitle from
Rose City to Knowledge City. I do not know if Mayor Rieger
was responsible for this or not.

Palmerston North sports a teachers' college and a university, plus the Universal College of Learning, the International Pacific College *and* the Adidas Institute of Rugby.
Knowledge City probably wasn't any one person's idea.

Palmerston North is the spiritual home of stockcar racing in New Zealand. The local team, the Palmerston North Panthers, have won 18 of the 39 titles since Team Champs were introduced in 1981. In that inaugural year, the Panthers came third behind inaugural winners
Palmerston North B.

Lots of famous people come from Palmerston North.
Alan Gregg, bass player with popular band the Mutton Birds, was once asked if he had roots in jazz. He replied that he had roots in Palmerston North.

I have often wanted to use that joke myself, and last week I got the opportunity when someone asked me where I thought I was coming from.

I come from Palmerston North. We are a modest people, but we are fiercely proud of the bustling, go-ahead city at the heart of the Manawatū Plains.

In sci-fi movies, people often go back in time in order to try to change history. This is impossible. You cannot change the past. And nobody from Palmerston North
would want to.

University Open Day

English was the uncoolest: awkward people
reading Shakespeare in a room.
We got trapped, but managed to get out
before the poetry started.

Food Tech was okay, with fresh bread
dyed to look mouldy, and bright blue juice
that it was easy to guess was lemon.
You could buy cans of air, too.

There was a long queue at Chemistry
because you got to make potions.
One of the white-coats
came rushing out in a real lather.

Psychology had us reading
a short paragraph describing 'Mr Smith',
then answering questions about his
personality. Opinions divided neatly.

The trick turned out to be a single word.
Some paragraphs described Mr Smith
as 'warm', others as 'cold'.
The psychologists beamed cleverly.

'Applied commonsense,' snorted a man
wearing a *Microbiologists*
            are Little Buggers T-shirt.
Outside, padded eggs were being dropped

from a rooftop. Engineering.
People kept saying Vet was best.
It had the cow with the glass panel.
Actually, the panel wasn't that interesting,

sort of dark and red. The cow
was eating hay in a small concrete room.
Mostly it just ate, but now and then
it would look sadly round at everyone,

and that's when I got to thinking
about Philosophy.
The department wasn't easy to find.
It turned out to be a single office

down a badly lit corridor.
A faded note on the door said
'Back in 10'. And so
my education began.

My Flatmate

My flatmate is an artist.
He says that making art
is all about preparation and focus,
so that you're always ready
for whenever inspiration
strikes.

He reckons it's a lot like
watching test cricket
—all too easy to be looking
the wrong way at the
crucial delivery. Apparently,
just tuning in to the highlights

is no substitute
for watching every ball.
I like listening to him
because he's got a degree
in physics or phys ed
or something.

He's what some people call
a 'PhD postie', and he's full
of really out-of-it theories.
For example:
he always eats breakfast
before going to bed

in order to
save time in the mornings.
And he believes that mail delivery
is like an enormous work in progress
that he and other posties
the world over

are trying to perfect.
He says just crossing our road
can be quite a performance.
'But how do you know,' I say,
'that what you end up with
is art?' He says it's difficult

to explain to people who aren't
artists themselves, but that
it's like being in love—you just know.
'Oh,' I say, because I don't.
So he agrees to show me.
We begin with cornflakes.

The End of the Runway

The first weekend we went to Dad's
we did more things than we mostly did in a whole year.
He took us to the zoo, the park, the movies and tenpin bowling.
He cooked us something for dinner on Friday night,
but on Saturday he said 'Stuff it' and we had fish and chips,
which suited everybody.

On Sunday afternoon we had an hour to kill
before going back to Mum's, so we stopped off at
the end of the runway to watch the planes.
It was dusk and we could see the sets of lights stacked out
over the ocean as each plane fell into line.
They seemed to take forever to reach us.

We were in the car off to one side.
I remember how you used to be able to stand
right in the flight path, crouching and covering your ears
as the approaching lights grew into insects, then birds,
then tonnes of straining, shrieking metal
shook over your head.

Dad got out and went and stood against the mesh fence,
hands shoved in his jeans' pockets. He was tall and muscular,
and his outline stood solidly against the wind and sky.
My brother got bored and started playing the game where
he'd punch at my face with full force but miss by a whisker.
'You're jet trash,' he kept saying. 'Jet trash' was his favourite word.

Dad came back to the car, got in, and started the engine.
He over-revved as he reversed, sending sprays of gravel
against the fence. We hit the road toward Mum's.
No one spoke. The grey evening sky barrelled over the hills.
'So,' Dad said finally, 'how is your mother?'
'Okay,' said my brother, who was sitting in the front seat.

Then he burst into tears. Dad kept driving for a bit,
but my brother kept crying, so he pulled over.
He laid his head against the steering wheel. My brother
was really bawling, his small shoulders shrugging up and down
like he was trying to take off. Dad leaned over and pulled him
into an awkward hug, which only made him cry more.

'Son,' he kept saying, 'son.' Then he turned to me to see
how I was doing. I was concentrating on the fogged up world
out the fogged up window, but his wet, hopeless face
somehow found a way through and got deep inside me, and,
try as I might, I have never been able to shake it out
my whole life long.

Suburbs

What's so sub about the 'burbs?
Every secret ever told began here
and spread outwards like *The Sweet Porridge*.
Take the houses and their actionable improvements,
shuffled together like an estate agent's deck of cards.

Look twice at the small businesses
hunkered round intersections—Gold Luck Takeaways,
Gateway Dairy, Hair It Is—and always somewhere
a small sign offering 'Exotic Driftwood' or 'Advice'.
In the suburbs anyone can name their price.

Notice the inevitable trampoline out back, from where,
as another evening of lawns and cooking simmers down,
you can see a window contain a man's struggles
with a bra. Ah, now he has it and, rising and falling,
attends to himself in the mirror, before

disappearing . . . as you yourself have to,
because it's time for dinner
or just time to go inside and close the door,
then maybe a little telly before
the orange street lights . . .

The Book of Sadness

If you were expecting a weighty tome,
you'll be disappointed.
The Book of Sadness is actually
quite small—a manky paperback, in fact,
that will fit snugly in a pocket.

Perusing a dim alcove of a second-hand shop,
I latched on to it immediately.
It had seen many owners.
I spied your name, inked
in your careful, considered hand
—and my own scrawl, of course,
lurching like a drunken spider.

I wondered what page you'd got up to,
but there were so many folded corners
and abandoned bookmarks
it was impossible to tell.

I opened one at random and, yes,
the passage was bleak beyond conscience;
after each sentence, I could feel
my slim allotment of hope
draining into sand.
Indeed, it would not take much
of such 'wrung consequence'
to leave one
'foetal in the well's zero'.

At the counter I offered five dollars,
as the soft-pencilled price indicated.
'I'm sorry, but it's actually ten,'
said old Mr P. 'You see, it's signed.'
'But,' I mumbled, 'I'm the author.'
'Good for you,' said old Mr P quietly,
'good for you.'

The Unsuccessful

In many ways he would have been ideal.
He had a relevant qualification.
Some months before he had even spent a few days in our office,
at his own instigation, to gain work experience.

During that time he had been willing and eager,
and had picked things up quickly.
He'd gone about the menial tasks we'd given him
with a grateful enthusiasm.

He'd got on well with everyone.
He was punctual, presentable and had
a sense of humour.
That's important in our line of work.

When I saw that he'd applied, my heart sank.
I know this is unfair, but I felt angry toward him.
Nevertheless, we went through the interview process
in a fair and balanced manner.

Afterwards, he rang up wanting to know why.
I said the usual stuff about the large number of quality applicants.
He was calm and polite, and ended the call by saying
that he hoped the door wasn't completely closed.

I have only seen him on three occasions since:
once, sitting by himself on a park bench, and once
reading a notice in the Central Library. And the other day
I was stuck in traffic and there he was,

crossing the road, staring intently
at something up in the sky.

The Cost

The local Anglican church
offers the cheapest photocopying
in the neighbourhood
at ten cents a copy.

But for forty crumpled sheets
you are charged six dollars.
The embarrassed administrator
explains how it's ten cents for parishioners

and fifteen cents for . . . 'others'.
She jokes awkwardly about whether
this constitutes a prejudice
and says you can give what you have.

But you think the rule is fair enough:
you have to pay for your sins
and at fifteen cents a page
the rates remain competitive.

Netball Practice

Near the end of netball practice
Kirsten hefts a pass to Alice,
the dreamy girl, who, gazing out
across the empty asphalt,

through the mesh fence, perhaps,
into the clouds' blue-grey synapses,
turns back to the game
in time

to take the catch
with her face.
A moment's silence: then an explosion
of tears and snot, and her mum

in from the side like a shot—a parent
clearly well used to water treatment.
The coach at once turns on
Kirsten

—couldn't she see
Alice wasn't ready?—
at which Kirsten, too, dissolves.
Practice drizzles to a close.

'It wasn't really fair,'
I say to Anna later,
'to yell at Kirsten for passing.
Alice should have been watching.'

'But she couldn't yell at *her*,'
explains Anna, 'because her mum was there.'
And, yes, that's just the way it is.
Power is the hand that gives.

The dreamy girl will wake up to this
during the next away-from-home
while waiting, calling, screaming for the pass
that's never thrown.

Silent Night

After we have hugged and mouthed our 'Take cares',
I wade through static air to the house. Inside,
quiet reflects off stillness—the interior oddly angular
without Anna and Tessa to blur the distinctions.

I sit down and eyeball the silence.
My eyes sketch small, precise fields; my lips fuse together
in an economic downturn. The kitchen suddenly cubist,
I am a bad trip, the quintessential unsmiley face.

I become part of the silence. I open my head and let
the stillness in—like when you are in a car that plunges into a river
you should lower the window a fraction and watch the water rise
until equilibrium lets you open the door and start swimming.

The picture I don't want: three white faces
in a back seat, whanging toward Auckland's
oncoming tide of vehicles. 'New Zealand doesn't have traffic,
just cars on a road': my dad on New Zealand driving.

I get up. The fridge is pretty much empty, so I take
my brand new bag to the supermarket.
It is good following a list, moving through the aisles as if underwater.
Enrobed confectionary puckers up.

But carrying home the FMCGs,
I pass the school playground where, only the day before,
the girls and I swam over the grass
to the lifeboat and rescue.

Sometimes the future squares before me
as a bleak, super-heated landscape, through which I am walking,
emotions numbed to ritual, in search of
food and shelter for my family.

Try selling that to someone.

Garage

A flat tyre, Mrs Brown? No, I'm afraid
it's much more serious. It looks like
the propeller this time. Oh yes.

That means we'll have to
replace the balcony and baffle the snidges,
wouldn't you say, Pete? I'm afraid

it's not going to come cheap, Mrs B.
And those windows are definitely
going to need . . . cleaning.

Maintenance

Yes, we have a chain tool.
Allen sent us one he'd found because he said
you really shouldn't take on a mission like this
without a proper chain tool.

Good. O.
So now here we are halfway to goddamn nowhere
with our chain tool and our pump and three spare tubes
and tyre levers for Africa spread around us like

some sort of mad industrial picnic.
And is anybody laughing?
No.
It's like the Family Court.

And what about that shivering dog we passed
back there
on the shady side of the track?
I don't think its legs were working.

I mean, it didn't get up.
It looked like that portrait of Thomas Hardy
on the cover of his *Selected Poems*.
Don't you hate that sort of simile?

It's cold—freezing—even though it's sunny.
We've been riding through ice.
Funny how winter days can do that.
In winter, clouds must be like blankets.

Maybe that dog belongs to those guys we saw
wheeling the pig out on a bike?
But it looked like a family dog.
Out here it won't last the night.

Allen's surname is Key. At least that makes us laugh,
and we haven't really laughed since early April.
That was when Max told us the joke
about Rangers supporters.

Max is short for Maxwell, but that isn't his first name.
His first name is actually William.
My granddad was called Tim,
but his first name was actually Albert.

Max supports Partick Thistle. Partick, not Patrick.
They're a small Glasgow club and, unbelievably, I once
played football with another (*the* other?) Partick Thistle supporter,
Angus, whose granddad had actually played football *for the club.*

Angus was mates with the one guy in our team
I didn't really like; whose crap personality, in fact,
partly prompted me to exchange football
for mountain biking. I forget his name.

I've never been too good with names
but I remember faces. I'll call the SPCA later.
Poor kids on the sideline, if they were his.
Poor sidelined kids the world over.

Ah, that's got it. Now all we need to do is pump it up.
Right, the joke.
Why are Rangers supporters like ET?
Because they look like him.

The Year of the Mountain

for Dinah Hawken

It was the Year of the Mountain, and when Li Po realised there was no avoiding it he began to make preparations. He packed water, rice cakes and sugar cane. He visited his mother. Then, after waiting for nightfall, he set forth. At first nothing, then gradually the mountain began to rise up in astonishment until Li Po could feel its wonder beneath his feet and hands. Twice he stopped to rest and to gaze at the stars. When the first shades of dawn began to ease open the sky, Li Po unfolded a black sash from about his person and bound it over his eyes. He hummed softly to himself as his hands sought out each new foothold. By now it was the Year of the Bicycle, and the following day it would be the Year of Unpopular Poetry. Li Po was already in training.

A Great Day

for Frank Sargeson

After a stroll round Viaduct Basin,
I'm sure you'd have been

happier than even we,
in all our nationalistic glory,

to see the Aussie boat break like meringue,
and all those gold faces floundering

at a certainty even the hottest legal entourage
couldn't salvage.

I'll go further and entertain that
you'd have been equally content when it

happened to our lot,
if only to see all the rich red socks

getting hung out to dry.
Perhaps you'd also have understood why

taking a hammer to the Auld Mug
was as genuine an act of love

as anyone's ever shown it.
I'm sure sailing's fine work, if you can get it,

but—as you knew—most of us
are hard pushed enough

just keeping our hearts above water
and making it back to shore.

No Rest

Wake up facing wall.
Sound of rain battering roof.
Taste of cabbage in mouth.
Fall of limbs into clothes.
No milk.
No bread.
No power to fridge.
Grin of spider in bath.
Smell of cat shit in shower.
Laughter of empty coat hook.
Recall coat on work chair-back.
Sprint down floundering road.
Battering of rain on head.
Battering of rain on world.
Battering of hand on departing bus.
Arrival of traction engine.
Driver in no hurry due to battering rain.
War and Peace passed among passengers.
Battering of rain on eventual arrival.
Swipe entry to building.
Swipe entry to building.
Brush teeth with finger.
Cement smile to face.
Make wet joke to silent room.
Assume desk.
Spill tea.
Log-in 'rejected'.
Work 'unable to be retrieved'.
Gaze at computer with libellous intent.
Called in to boss for chat.
Hurried pulling up of socks.
Told to pick up pace.
Told to wake up ideas.
Told to pull up socks.
Resume desk.
Leave message with IT.
Try to hang up phone.

Try to pick up pieces.
Try to not cry.
Take stock.
Take deep breath.
Take running jump.
Thump computer.
Thump printer.
Thump stapler.
Thumb stapled to work station.
Stagger to sickbay.
Told to lose weight.
Told to gain confidence.
Told to relax.
Walk carefully to tearoom.
Make weak tea joke to back of queue.
Coincide with boss.
Smile through clenched toes.
Resume desk.
Leave message with IT.
Tip tea in pot plant.
Try to avoid meeting.
Try to avoid trouble.
Try to avoid void.
Seep of seconds into lunch hour.
Exit building via disused stairwell.
Coincide with boss.
Smile through clenched silence.
Eat scalding pie in rain-strewn doorway.
Eat scalding fingers in rain-strewn pie.
Eat strewn words in rain-scalded head.
Resume desk.
Leave message with IT.
Traipse into rudderless meeting.
Tapping of rain on window.
Tapping of finger on pen.
Tapping of words on brain.
Shake head.
Nod head.
Nod off.

Wake to posture sliding from chair.
Wake to improbable dreams involving team leader.
Wake to startling new punchline to Noddy joke.
Strive to ignore buzzing fluoro.
Strive to think of sensible question.
Strive not to tell Noddy joke.
Agree to differ.
Agree to compromise.
Agree to agree.
File out into endless corridor.
Resume desk.
Leave message with IT.
Visit toilet.
Coincide with boss.
Smile through clenched bottom.
Resume desk.
Draft dazzling letter of resignation.
Visit recycling bin.
Make small talk with stressed colleagues.
Make molehill out of mountain.
Make dart.
Resume desk.
Stick pin in desk mascot.
Look busy.
Look out of window.
Look into lost soul.
Leave message with IT.
Attempt work in hardcopy.
Work hard at copy attempt.
Copy attempt at work hard.
Ingest fumes from correction fluid.
Experience time as gelid ellipse.
Drip wobble of seconds into stupendous bullet points:
- Literacy practice is effective when it leads to
  improved literacy achievement
- Teacher efficacy is strongly related
  to being an effective teacher
- The poem is about the mind's ability
  to fashion for itself a series of problems

and thereby a series of possible solutions
- God is always greater than all our troubles

Find lost lucky penny.
Shut down computer.
Ha fucking ha.
Sprint down exit stairwell.
Forget coat.
Forget to buy milk.
Forget to learn from mistakes.
Catch world's most missable bus.
Crawl of nose against window.
Crawl of babies into adulthood.
Crawl of snails into advanced species.
Battering of rain on bus.
Battering of rain on suburbs.
Battering of rain on rain.
Sprint up floundering road.
Collect sodden demands from letterbox.
Climb 4000 steps to front door.
Stare at key through locked window.
Contort back through stuffed toilet louvres.
Seek illumination from 40 watt bulb.
Seek sustenance from reheated dinner.
Seek picture in snow on telly.
Try to make bed to lie in.
Try to make light of day.
Try to make light of darkness.

The Wicked

It starts at the edge of your teeth
like a small stone caramelised within a black jellybean,
and then it is grinding inside you like a cancer.
How can you write words you can't even splutter,
that you can barely even think,
your mind an unspeakable furnace,
your tongue forever tripping over the neighbour's cat?
You can't find a fucking pen
in the whole fucking house that works
and, when you do, anger leads you nowhere.
But you follow, oh how you follow,
suddenly hearing the voice of that appalling poet
who once told you how he sent his books to schools
with a note saying they had ten days to return them
before his invoice would arrive. 'It's often easier,'
he'd confided, 'for busy librarians to write out a cheque
than to repackage the book and return it.'
You'd wanted to pull his miserable beard out
there and then. You count calmly to ten
then go about resetting the rat poison without
a moment's consideration for the neighbour's cat.
You feel a wonderful power 'surging' through you.
Clichés feed your strength because
you've got a one-way ticket to hell
and you don't care. Fire rages, clouds scud.
On your bike you weave and spit
a throaty, viral gob over the windscreen
of an SUV that won't give way.
There is no rest for the wicked in this world.
At night you bully the dishes
into some sort of submission
before reading the kids a super scary story
—though you are the one tormented by nightmares
of terrible things befalling them.
On the news, the pain and hatred between
the Palestinians and the Israelis are exemplary.
From a distance it's plain how senseless it all is,

and how nobody can win, but you can feel the anger
and frustration seething inside you,
and you know you'd be out there,
telling yourself the old lie about
how it's because you love your home
and family more than life itself
that you can feel your fist rising
against the armour
in another offensive headline,
your partner wailing at the news,
your children's indescribable faces
howling into the cycle.

The Time of Your Life

The turn of the century.
            The dawn of the decade.
The year of the cockerel.
            The winter of our discontent.
The summer of love.
            The age of Aquarius.
The ides of March.
            The moment of truth.
The nick of time.
            The knell of parting day.
The twilight of the gods.
            The end of an era.
The twinkling of an eye.
            The chance of a lifetime.

A night of it.
            A term of endearment.
A momentary lapse of reason.
            A fraction of a second.
A stitch in time.
            A minute of silence.
An hour of darkness.
            A day of shame.
A period of mourning.
            A month of Sundays.
Oh season of mists . . .
            Two shakes of a lamb's tail.
Fifteen minutes of fame.
            One hundred years of solitude.

The Bike Lesson

1. Body and Bike

As violins are singing trees, a bicycle
  is an orchestra of the body.
On song, movement begets
  balance and balance
   begets movement:
strings, woodwinds, brass, percussion
   navigating the waves of air, earth, water
    —all the arguing terrains—
to arrive, flushed and fizzing,
  at the mouths of
   all the arguing
    inner ears.
Cleaned, lubed and wiped
  to within a sheen of conception,
   or tossed like a bad hand,
  an untenanted bicycle
   equals
  a tenanted motor vehicle
—strength without muscle,
  bravery without courage,
   beauty without heart.
The drivetrain (an essential element)
  can be refined
   beyond the visible
by a body's bellowing lungs
   and resonant angles,
  till it pings like love
    in the open air.
  But not always.
What would life be
  with the injustice of always?
Is a body always heavenly?
  Are today's legs any good?
Will today's fluids gain or reduce traction?
  Is today's mind such that

today doesn't matter?
        Sometimes a bell is necessary . . .
The lure of sport, games
        and reality TV
                is our secular prayer
        for a simplified, playable
                world,
where there is, nonetheless,
        no telling
                the tuning
beyond the progress of the piece:
        the granny gear,
                the terrifying big ring,
                        the final whistled section.

2. The Tip Track

You have to do the work. And mostly it isn't poetry.
        It's time to bike up a hill.
Have a glass of water and shoulder up
        your too-heavy backpack.
Ride the 3.9 km round the road to the bottom
        —a warm-up for whatever's about to fry.
Don't overdo it into the inevitable wind,
        just get the legs ticking over,
reminding them. As you approach the bottom,
        chop down into the gear
you want to start in (1.3?). At the main gate
        take a brief moment to acknowledge
the half hour of hell ahead. Breathe easy.
        Sip your water and lemonade mix.
Check you're in the right gear and wearing
        minimal layers. Right,
don't focus too long or reason will cloud your vision.
        Click the timer and push those legs.
Up the first bit, staying left, over the small gulch
        and round the gate through the gap on the right.
Change up a gear for the brief flat bit over the soft ground

and flowing s's where water has snaked a course.
Stay hard left past the s's, then surge into the climb,
        hitting the middle-left bedrock.
Chop down to 1.2, your basic climbing gear.
        Somewhere here, the pain begins.
Now there's a brief reduction in gradient
        with the track moving left and the best line
middle-right as the first attack stretches up before you.
        The track is badly washed out left and right:
the best approach is a narrow line up the middle.
        Yep, it's narrow, steep and bumpy,
so you need to hold good momentum to avoid stalling
        into the rocky channels left and right.
But it's early days and you have the claws. Over the concrete
        pipe—bump—and you're doing fine.
Now the gradient eases briefly; the channel meanders
        in the middle and you meander over it to the right,
up a short, scrabbly incline, and must cross it again to the left.
        It's a rockier gulf, but cross early and relax
onto the smoother surface as the gradient increases again.
        The channel waggles ahead of you
and you must recross to return to the right as the track steepens
        and swings into a left bend. Cross early . . . or late
where the channel weaves over to the inside track of the corner.
        You're on clay now and it's suddenly steep.
Sidle up right, across the track, and, as a new channel cuts back across,
        enjoy a (very) brief levelling. Stay hard right
and bump over the channel, hitting it straight on at its source,
        and you're straight into an attack up a steep, clay incline.
Lean hard into it—out of the saddle—then ease off
        as the track bears left and pushes up right
onto a less-steep, but longer and lumpier clay incline.
        Stay hard right, right handlebar punching past gorse,
or move middle to avoid the worst bumps. The incline weakens
        and the surface improves, the lumps gone.
Keep right as the track curves left, then straightens right.
        Things level onto a short, flat bit before rising into
a short, steep climb snaked with mild channels. The best line is right,
        with a welcome mat of fine, packed gravel to ease off onto.

The incline weakens again as the track meanders easily
       right then left then right for the longest stretch of relief yet.
Enjoy, but keep left as there's a sudden, ugly, washout
       on your right! You're now approaching the quarter-way bend
—a big left-hander that you can either round far right (tired)
       or by taking the shorter, steeper, middle route.
The middle offers smooth bedrock and you want to be far left
       for the smoothest ascent line anyway. Breathe well
and get your legs into a rhythm as the steep but consistent gradient
       and reasonable surface allow for it.
Now there's another brief levelling dip before the gradient resumes.
       Cross over to your right in the dip and move far right
as a treacherous middle rut starts to cut nearer to you.
       The rut is forcing you far right and, just before
the gradient briefly levels again, you have to cross it.
       Attack it straight on as it peters to its source, hit the flat bit
and round the corner middle-right. Once round, move left.
       The gradient eases and surface becomes dirt.
The track swings right with you staying left. A rough, rocky, steeper
       bit now. Attack middle or left but bear left.
Stay left as the incline decreases again and the track swings left
       then right toward another rocky steeper bit.
Again, attack middle but bear left. Again, the track swings
       left, right, left. The surface becomes loose bedrock
and steepens before straightening into another moderately steep,
       sustained incline—clay with scattered rocks.
Attack middle or left, keep those legs working, and stay left.
       The gradient eases on the top left bend; stay hard left,
taking the inside track, pushing up again on the bedrock.
       This final up is easy, but hurts because you're reaching
the top of the first half of climbing! Urrrggghhh!
       Now the incline lessens considerably onto easy gravel:
a final hump and you're on a cake-walk gradient for a couple of
       minutes as you close in on the stockyards and HALFWAY.
Either recharge or charge—up to 1.3, 1.4, 2.1, 2.3 . . . !
       Enjoy the view back to your right, the snaking incline
you've just climbed, its vibrant gorse and barberry.
       Is this the lost poetry? No, sadly, and worse is to come.
Poo, that smell is gas being burnt off at the tip!

Pick the smoothest bedrock lines in the middle or inside
track on corners. Now the gradient levels out properly
    and the track purrs left towards the stockyards.
A hard-right turn past a post and you're roughly HALFWAY.
    It's time for a time check.
If you're under 15 minutes and not shattered
    you should make the road in under 30
—which means, according to the Kennetts, that you're fit!
    Praise the baby Lord Jesus!
You should now be in 2.3, 2.4, 2.6 . . . (your body will let you know)
    as you sail *down* over the gravel stockyards towards
the next short up (2.2, 2.1). Pushing hard for the next few minutes
    as the track bobs and sidles towards a saddle
will gain you more time for less energy than blowing out on steep bits.
    The track bobs up again, then down (2.3, 2.4), then
up (2.2, 2.1), then down, then up, before a longer downhill (2.7, 2.8!)
    towards a sharp, blind right-hander. Bellow 'BIKE',
a downhiller could be bombing down the other way. As you round
    the bend, you're approaching another short uphill
(often into the wind), where you'll quickly be chopping down.
    The sharp turn off to your left drops down into Spooky Gully.
Now you're breasting the ascent's longest downhill—two swoops
    curving left that invite you to use the full width of track
for the best line through the gate. Change up and pedal!
    Watch out for the loose gravel (and winter puddle)
at the bottom of the saddle as you level out and sail
    left then right into the second half of the climb.
Chop down quickly—2.7, 2.6, 2.5, 2.4, 2.3, 1.3—and hope
    you don't lose your chain! The sudden incline
quickly decreases and is a bit rocky but almost level.
    You could change up here and push it,
but you'll probably feel best in 2.1 or 1.3 as you plod round
    a big right-hand bend (which affords you becalmed views
of the saddle and previous swoops) because you need to
    conserve your strength for the CRUEL TESTS ahead.
Now the surface becomes dirt and the gradient gradually increases
    as the track paws left. Grit your mind, the next 5 minutes
are the toughest. The track continues to bear left and,
    although the surface is still dirt, the rocks are increasing.

157

Stay left—the first test will loom up on a blind, left-hand bend.
A big water channel is opening on the right. Breathe deep.
Move middle to take advantage of the washed clay surface on the bend.
The gradient steepens—take the left (inside) track and attack!
The surface on the left is hard-packed and gives good grip.
Only a short surge is required, but you'll still be sweating!
Stay focused as the surface becomes marbles. Breathe deep,
for although the gradient lessens you've
virtually no recovery time before the track swings right
into the second, and HARDEST, test.
The surface quickly deteriorates into large, loose rocks.
Stay left, start attacking early and don't let up! The bend
swings blind left, like the last one, but the surface is appalling
and the gradient steeper for longer. The water channel
is again on the right, but you're hugging hard left, maybe in 1.1,
taking an inside track. This is steeper than an outside line,
but offers the firmest surface. Get your weight forward
and keep your momentum up. No way is this poetry.
Attack that inside line! Spin firm but even, you don't want to slip.
As the narrow line of solid surface vanishes under loose rocks,
bounce straight out into the middle of the track to make the left turn
(the rut on the right has vanished into rubble).
The surface is total crap—large, loose rocks—
so you'll need solid momentum to maintain balance
should your back wheel skid. Luck and strength
have to combine here, for, making the left turn, you
have scant spare speed for slippage. When the back tyre grips, surge
and bounce over the loose rocks and up the brief bedrock apex.
Now the gradient improves, but you're still going up on loose change.
But you've just made the HARDEST BIT,
so don't lose it now just because your lungs are punching
your tonsils. How bad do you want it?
The track swings right towards the third test, which isn't hard, but,
because of its proximity to the torturous second test,
looms before you like a sick joke. It's straight—part boulder,
part bedrock—and you can attack it either straight on,
taking a left-hand line, or by weaving right over boulders
and then back left (the less daunting option).
The point is you're gasping and although the gradient

isn't steep, even the less-direct route will twist the knife.
Once up the third test, you've a couple of bends of easy, grassy surface
and (almost) level gradient on which to recover.
They are, however, punctuated by a loose, rocky left-hand bend
with a tight left-hand line, which can unseat you,
especially now you're tired. Stay focused, and push hard left.
Alternatively, round it far right then middle.
If you slip on the loose stuff, pedal! Stay strong
as the almost-level grassy bit resumes and the gradient
increases towards the fourth test. This is a rocky, left-hand bend
followed by a straight, rocky incline into another
left-hand bend. Approach the first left-hander on the left, but
surge into the middle as you make the turn.
Ride up the straight on the left-hand side.
The gradient isn't as steep as tests one and two,
and although the surface is strewn with rocks
there are plenty of good lines.
A bedrock hump on the second left-hand turn marks the top.
There are multiple lines here too: for example,
hard left or middle through a small cleft in the bedrock.
Now the track really does LEVEL OUT
before the fifth test, but your recovery time is short
as the rocks grow into boulders and multiply quickly.
Ahead you can see the track jink into a sharp, right-hand turn
followed by a short, steep attack.
Although short, this is the Tip Track's steepest angle.
The trick is to keep wanting it and attack *before* the rise.
A good approach line is important here because the right-hand turn
is strewn with large, loose rocks. Generally,
it's best to approach the turn from the right, crossing
to the left to actually make the turn and attack!
Sometimes there is also a decent approach line on the right
(the inside track). One good thing: because the slope
is hard-packed grit (waiting to wash out) and bedrock, you can,
for the moment, attack it anywhere. Good momentum
is always the key to the short and steep, which is why
hitting a boulder on approach and slipping can be fatal here.
Once up the fifth test, CONGRATULATIONS, you have essentially
cleaned the Tip Track! Power on (or take it easy)

up the straight, bedrock gradient, enjoying the bouncy grip,
      and swing round a blind left-hand corner.
But stay awake: although the gradient levels, the sudden swath
      of loose gravel can still surprise you.
Keep left as the (now) dirt surface swings right then left
      towards the Red Rocks junction.
You've stayed left because the mud surface has allowed
      a channel to open on the right. At the junction
you need to cross this because you're turning right for the final assault.
      It's a straight, right-angle crossing—power through at the
obvious place. Your time at this point needs to be about 27 minutes
      if you want to break the golden 30, because it'll take you
another couple to reach the gate—and then you've got to
      reach the sealed road. Leaving the junction, stay right
as the rocky track bears mild right towards a slightly steeper
      left bend. There's a plot of loose rocks—the source
of the rocky rut on the left—so clinging to the right-hand side
      and being forceful over the top is the most direct route.
Then it's over a gulch and up a short, steep bit into the left-hander.
      Stay right and pick the best lines as you sprint for the top.
There are a couple more drainage gulches, which you'll
      scarcely notice now that you can see the gate.
Keep right as you approach because it's possible to squeeze
      your bike through the gap between the gate
and pole on the right. Do so, taking care to unclip cleanly,
      and slip through yourself. Your legs will die on you,
so swearing and determination are the keys to keeping 20 seconds
      off your time. Getting back on here really hurts
—sod the sealed-road rule. Teeter into your saddle. If you clip in,
      great, but there's no room to faff about if you don't,
no space to pick a line (hard right is best), you just need
      immediate momentum. Charge. Push for the road,
bouncing sharp left over the verge of grass and tussock.
      YOU'RE THERE! Stop the clock. Fall from bike
. . . or change up to 2.2 and enjoy a leisurely warm-down
      up the sealed road to the summit.
The view is to die for and you probably feel like it.
      Why on earth are you doing this?
You could be at home kicking back and reading poetry.

Ah, but poetry is sometimes about suffering.
The trig height is 495 metres. The Tip Track record
      (bottom gate to sealed road)
is 20 minutes flat set by Simon Kennett in 1997.
      Bear in mind that the track is graded every few years
and was in reasonable, 'misty' condition at the time.
      Also, wind can add at least a couple of minutes
to an ascent—a southerly is the most advantageous direction
      for climbing, but no wind is best.
Except if it's hot. The Tip Track in blazing summer heat
      is a bad idea—which is why you're carrying
at least 2 litres of water, not to mention food, coat, tools, etc
      (open heart, light head), for you've
other places to get to.   This is just the beginning.

3. *The Top*

All the best weather happens
      above 500 metres.
One unparticular day,
      sky grey and rising,
            a light sugar
turned our attention to pointillism
      until we realised
            it was snowing.
It was 19 September, Makara Peak, south Karori.
      Small groups wheeled in
            the daffy, sunstruck air,
mouths opening and closing
      on the simple
            complex.
What way is there
      to do justice
            to reaching
all-points-down
      under your own exchange?
What stares back at you?
      Do you become

bigger or smaller?
Once, from the golfball, I waved toward our
tiny mustard dot
in Island Bay
where, at a prearranged time,
Catherine, Anna and Tessa
stared through binoculars
at what I hoped
was me.

4. *The Downhill*

What I like about rain
is its gravity.
What goes up, must come down,
may not be
rocket science,
but the perfecting of it
is.
Descent is the straight line
between
crescendo and nightmare.
Welcome to the fast . . . the flow,
like water over impediment,
narrowing the air's gasps.
It's about being slightly
out of control ;
each thimble shift in weight
refining the line
dividing
cadence and catastrophe;
every
nip and tuck
through each declining
contour
popping
the inner ear
with a new definition

                of justice.
Or, because velocity is not free, the other
            ever-present scenario: the hard
                                    slap
and full stop of
            move
                        ment.

5. *Pear-shaped*

Where did last year's lessons go?
            Be honest, sometimes you are
                        pushing the envelope
when it folds in on you;
            trying to ride
                        through custard
                                    as it turns to it;
            out on a limb
                        when it

But other times
            it falls like fish
                        from clear blue sky.
Too much speed, not enough . . .
            Would hindsight really be
                        a wonderful thing,
                                    or plain boring?
After all, there is no foretelling
            the ground effect.
Too much speed, not enough . . .
            You curl into a ball;
you bounce or burst or break
                        your fall;
            your mind's returned,
                        marooned
                                    or called.
Step into the light
                        poor Lazarus.

6. Why We Do What We Do

You have to do the work.
　　　　And mostly it isn't poetry.
The big question is always why.
　　　　Necessity? Pleasure?
　　　　　　　Obligation? Enlightenment?
　　　　Biology? Pressure?
　　　　　　　Culture? Entanglement?
Narrative desire? A means to an end?
　　　　　　　Error? Accident?
　　　　Challenge? Bewilderment?
Sorry. This is where you get off.
　　　　I missed generosity
　　　　　　　and plain old good-heartedness.
　　　　Needs build their own houses.
It is superb in the air.
　　　　The light is streaming in
　　　　　　　and I want to be out in it
(which is never as easy as it sounds).
Like you, I have had disappointments.
　　　　I write mostly for my shelf.
If there's something
　　　　you want to hear,
you can sing it
　　　　　　　yourself.

from *Warm Auditorium*

Work Station

If I had a window, I would look out of it.
The sun's reflections on puddled concrete
would brighten my eyes.

The woman planting a kiss
would remind me of touch and spring growth
and the daily importance of clichés.

And the man with groceries
trying to cross the road to his family
would no longer escape my attention.

'Look,' I would announce,
'there is his youngest daughter, who has knelt down
to help him tie his shoelace.'

How I Write My Love Poems

Dry rain: all day I break rules.
First, the rule of law, then
the law of diminishing returns.
Finally, confounded by grammar,
I head for the hills.
Maybe there are no obligations now.
Veins inhabit the mind like supplejack.
There's a point where your exertion enters
its own personal funnel and sound mummifies,
the way a shell presses the sea to an ear.
Is it not truly something how you can hear
small points of light emerging from the brightness?
The law of combining volumes
is rewritten as we speak.
Chance fattens like an ambulance until,
breasting a widow's peak, the heart upholds
its tall story. You're on top of the world
—hair you can upbraid, personal
pronouns you take for your own.
And, further into the zone:
sudden delicious Braille, a ribcage's
brimming xylophone, the unwritten
rules of engagement
making a home.

Thirst

Let the grumblers move to Australia
—who wants to live somewhere so dry
you have to drink your own urine?
My sister comes in from the lounge,
fills a glass with water, and goes back again.
Not drinking enough is one cause of
kidney stones, which then need to be 'dissolved' or
'passed', often causing a 'burning sensation'.
In the lounge, a log has rolled from the fire
igniting the hearth mat.
My sister comes back for another glass of water.
By the time the Snorkel arrives, the fire chief says
our house is 'fully involved'.
It almost starts to rain, some droplets swirling
in the orange streetlights.
I need the loo, and am sent next door.
Old Mr Sandbar is still helping his wife
(who died years ago) out of the bath.
I get into a staring competition with
a bikini babe in an Aussie holiday brochure.
If I lose, she will dive into the lagoon
and exchange my eyes for pearls.
If I win, I will go blind.

Click Here for Title

'Reality is merely that which you can be persuaded of'
announced my frightening but ineffectual Lit Crit lecturer one day.
I wasn't convinced. Back then, which of us was?
A leggy, sophisticated classmate, with an almost ugly mouth
that I thought beautiful (though I knew even then
that was a cliché of romantic fiction), smiled conspiratorially.
Am I on the inside looking out or the outside looking in,
is a non-question I still ask myself. Also, why is my poetry
so prosy? She seemed so together, but years later
had some sort of breakdown. By then poetry
was running round my head like marbles over linoleum.
The twentieth century departed.
I thought there was nothing I could do.
Money can buy what you want,
but it can't buy wanting it.

The Glistener

I glisten to people all day.
Everything they say is true.
By night I am beside myself.

Eventually, the house across the street goes silent.
In the head hours, I go outside and look about me.
The moon lowers its fine lace fabric over the suburb.
Condoms prevent STDs, but they break the dream.
Plus, you know what's going to happen next.

Once, I made love to a woman I didn't care for.
Once, I spat at someone
and was thrown to the ground.
Once, I called my youngest child a nuisance.

'Action causes more trouble than thought.'
I am tiny in starlight.

Long Shadows

She loses her virginity down the garden
in the onion weed
under the crabapple.

She leaves town for the city;
reappears on regional TV.

The freckle astride her left breast
is a partially developed third nipple,
she explains, reaching for her ankle.

One morning, cloven hoof prints
pock the planter on her
sixth floor balcony.

In her defence,
she elects not to swear on the Bible.
She lies on her bed
watching the light babble.

The grey afternoon returns
to the suburbs, the provisional;
the crabapple gone to infill,
the onion weed still hanging in there

between the rusted tricycle
and clawed bath full of bottles
the current tenants mean to recycle.

The Worst Job in the World

My dad did it. He went to a place
where vans come and collect the men
who want to work. Sometimes
they mowed grass in the middle of roundabouts
or cut scrub along the motorway.
But one day they got taken to the docks.
They got given sponges and plastic buckets.
The job was to go inside the empty tanks
of a supertanker and soak up the oil
the pumps couldn't get.
My dad, he didn't want to do it, but
he was miles from home and there was
no ride back if he didn't work.
So he went to the gear pile,
but there were no more overalls.
Tough $#î+! At the end of the day
his clothes had to be thrown away.
All of his pay went on new jeans.
I asked him what it was like
at the bottom of a supertanker,
but I can't put what he said because it is
Not Appropriate For The Classroom.
When I grow up I want to work for Mitsubishi
and go on their Christmas float.

What the Very Old Man Told Me

That he had regrets. That he didn't like saying
things were better in the old days,
but they probably were.
That God existed, but only as an idea.

That most people had rocks for brains.
That Wordsworth was right about emotion
recollected in tranquility, but wrong about nature.
That one should never turn one's back on the sea.

That vehicles shouldn't be allowed on beaches.
That I should be careful about shellfish.
That he liked form. That his joints ached
when it was overcast.

That asked to choose between the devil and
the deep blue sea, he'd take the deep blue sea.
That Roger and Simon were his favourite characters
in *Lord of the Flies*.

That automatic cars were hopeless
because you couldn't crash start them.
That his jet-ski cuff-links were a present
from one of his sons. That they were a joke.

That the mind is first a maze, then a treadmill.
That he preferred classical music.
That dogs should never have thrown
their lot in with humans.

That he could barely recall
the strange young man who wrote
<u>Daddy</u> *from the author* *9/4/37*
in his book *Enemies: Poems 1934–36.*

That he missed glass milk bottles.
That he loved his wife.
That he liked walking.
That he liked watching water.

Stan and the Cellphone

'I'm frightened,' I say. 'Please can you tell me a story.'
'Dude,' says my bro, 'OK. Which one d'you want?'
'Stan and the Cellphone,' I say, because I am always texting.
'OK,' says my bro. I hear him settling himself in the dark.
'This guy called Stan goes into a bar.'
'Do you know Stan?' I ask. 'Sure,' says my bro.
'So it's a true story?' I ask. 'I guess,' says my bro.
The darkness surrounds us. 'Anyway,' he says,
'Stan is sitting at the bar and in walks this gorgeous chick.'
'Like Lady Gaga?' I say. 'Naa, like drop dead gorgeous.'
'Like Angelina Jolie?' I say. 'Naa, more Lara Croft
with the Nude Raider patch if you insert the jewel on level 15.'
There's a pause in which we both think about Lara Croft
with the Nude Raider patch if you insert the jewel on level 15.
At least that's what I think about. I don't really know
what my bro thinks about.
'Anyway, Stan and the gorgeous chick, they get chatting.'
'But,' I interrupt, 'what Stan doesn't know is his cellphone
in his jeans' pocket has turned on and dialled the first number
in his contacts—which is his girlfriend.'
'Who's telling this story?' says my bro.
'Sorry,' I say. 'He must be wearing tight jeans.'
'The tightest. Stan is one cool dude.'
I try to imagine Stan's jeans.
'But his girlfriend ain't home,' says my bro.
'Lucky for him,' I say. 'Not,' says my bro,
'cos her answerphone is—and it starts recording.
When she gets home, she listens to the messages
and, whammo, does she go ballistic!'
'So she hears the whole conversation?' 'Most of it.'
'And the sound quality was good enough?' 'Most of it.'
'Even in a bar?' 'It's noisy, but she can hear Stan's voice
chatting up the chick clear enough. Then Stan comes home.'
'What happens?' I say. 'You know the rest,' says my bro.
'Please,' I say. 'I'm frightened.' My bro sighs.
'OK. Stan comes home and they fight and she forgives him.'
'Are they still together?' I say. 'Yeah,' says my bro.

'Do you think . . . ?' I say. 'Go to sleep,' says my bro.
I do an experiment I sometimes do.
I close my eyes in the darkness and then open them
to see if I can hear a difference. And tonight I can.

My Oatmeal Granddaughter

Walking home from school she flits
backwards, dallies sideways.
She stops to gentle seeds and snails,
her brow all over miles and furrows.
She is silence for hours, then bright shoals
fulfil her mouth and eyes.
Lost worlds are her room and hair.
I see her hugging the air, talking to Lego.
Loud noise and she surrounds her ears.
She runs mooing from the evening news, croons
'The Jolly Miller' over and all.
She is a shooting star, without friends or resistance,
but I firmly believe that in one future
some great instance
will shine from her.

Dan Chiasson

I've never written in a way that really pleases James.
    He likes my poem 'XV. Randall Jarrell',

from my second book *Natural History,*
    and has even used it as a writing exercise,

but not one of my other poems stays with him.
    'Randall Jarrell' is not a poem I care for, particularly.

Its cleverness sounds too 'creative writing course'—which it isn't.
    I'm pleased James likes it, even though I find myself questioning

his judgement given that he seems unable to discern the merits
    of some of my better poems. It's the old seesaw:

authorial intention versus reader response, and the puzzle of why we
    seem to value external approval above our own incantations.

I know my poetry isn't likely to win awards or find its way
    into great anthologies, and yet I keep writing it.

Have I come to terms with my mediocrity
    or let my dreams fly away? It's the wrong question.

I know what James is thinking, but he still has much to learn,
    especially about conclusions.

The Trialist

for Andrew Clarke

He's introduced as Jimmy, and so we call him
Sheep. A doe-eyed, jumped-up hopeful from
a failed, woolly colony, he's here on
a month's trial. I've seen so many come

and go
dreaming of Ronaldinho.
He hasn't a shit show.
Who of his countrymen have made a go

of the Premier League? Lord Nelsen
captains Blackburn,
but he's a defender—has mastered the art of getting in
the way—this lamb fancies his name on

the score sheet. First practice,
we shut him down, the tackles less and less
forgiving, until he asks what gives, says he's
on our side. Is he thick? His bleat receives

my back, but Big Rob's in his ear:
'Ah don't care who ya're or where
ya from, ya not coming here
an' takin' ma job. Do ah make masalf clear?'

So it goes for three grim weeks. But it must be Year
of the Ram. Injury, suspension and a career-
ending 'off-field incident' take their
toll, and, come Saturday, the Governor

has him on the bench. It's nil–nil
halfway through the second spell
when the Gov gambles on a double
change, pushing for the win, the critical

three points dangling before him like a snare.
Then, a wrong foot: Big Rob—heart of steel, head of air—
collects a second yellow in a rash attempt at flair.
The Gov avoids the Chairman's stare.

A mad reshuffle and the sheep shagger is on
—alone up front where he can do least harm.
We hardly even yell at him,
ignoring his distant, waving arm,

his incisive runs to nowhere,
instead turning the ball back or square.
Twice I delay a pass to where
he madly gestures

so he's caught offside. See, that's precisely why
you'll never pull a wage in this league, sonny.
Then sod me
if he doesn't score a beauty.

Gets on to a nothing ball, skips past
his man and bangs it in . . . to our collective gasp.
After that, some passes start
to find him. I even offer up a smart

one-two. When the final whistle goes
I'm at his side for photos,
helping him acknowledge the applause
and negotiate the post-match media whores.

'The team dug deep today,' I say. 'The Gov's punt
paid off. It was tough for Jim alone up front,
but we were always in the hunt,
and he latched on to a chance and made it count.

He's a good lad, with a great turn of speed.
The boys've rallied round to help him find his feet
and they'll make sure he keeps
them on the ground this coming week.'

The Green Plastic Toy

Four days into the much-vaunted schist landscape,
what claimed the fullest attention of my brother and I
was the green plastic toy.
Among the fractured outcrops and weathered columns,
the green plastic toy held sway.
The green plastic toy was never an 'it'.
Nor was the green plastic toy ever announced by
an indefinite article.
The green plastic toy was unique.
The greenness of the green plastic toy
was of a hue not to be found anywhere
within the spectrum of the surrounding nature.
The surface of the green plastic toy had not been
dulled, altered or encumbered
by the relentless forces of wilderness in any way.
Had the green plastic toy fallen from heaven?
During rest and meal breaks, my brother and I
could not wait to unpack the green plastic toy.
I wanted to play with the green plastic toy,
but my brother felt the green plastic toy
should only be placed somewhere,
on a rock or something, and admired.
Consequently, my brother and I sometimes
fought over the green plastic toy.
Consequently, we were made to share
the green plastic toy by our father.
Both of us maybe worshipped the green plastic toy.
Both of us maybe coveted the green plastic toy
for ourselves.
Both of us maybe bestowed upon the green plastic toy
a secret pet-name which we kept from the other.
When we left the much-vaunted schist landscape
and returned home, our father told us to place
the green plastic toy carefully
in the special treasure drawer, and to leave it be.
And so many years passed, with neither of us making
any claim for the affections of the green plastic toy.

Then, one day, I opened the special treasure drawer
in pursuit of another matter, and noticed
the absence of the green plastic toy.
I accused my brother, who accused me
of having invented the theft of the green plastic toy
in order to get back at him over some past grievance.
'See,' he said, pulling open the special treasure drawer
and drawing forth a mere pounamu,
'here is the green plastic toy.'
I saw that he spoke the truth for, in his practised hand,
the mere pounamu had indeed become
the green plastic toy, which swung
and shimmered as he advanced toward me
declaiming things about our past relationship
in a language I no longer understood.

Rungs and Daggers

Deep as a puddle I am and twice as useless.
One day I got the position, bent to adjust my kit and
by the time I straightened up my youngest child was 14.
That is one thing I have learned and here are some others:

- If you run forward when you are defending,
  you may find the ball sailing over your head
  to the person you were supposed to be marking.
- In netball, which everyone should play at least once,
  if you bat at the ball with one hand
  you will almost certainly fail to catch it, and a jabbing ponytail
  will almost certainly be in to snatch it.
- In football, forwards love goalkeepers who bat.
- If you are a goalkeeper, and a forward is coming at you
  unimpeded, you must come out and try to intercept them,
  even though the ball could go sailing in over your head.
- To improve, you must almost always be
  in over your head.
- Dreams mostly begin in dreams, which you will naturally follow
  until, one skied sitter too many, you're persuaded that the midfield
  better suits your 'football brain', before lack of touch and pace
  see your arm perpetually raised in a lugubrious, Arsenalesque
  defence, goose-stepping forward as one.
- Finally, the loneliest position. Goalkeeper.
  There is no one behind you on this one.
  In the social leagues, no net even, and you have to scramble
  down banks of despairing foliage,
  past stripped cars and items of clothing
  of interest to police, until you come to a clearing
  littered with the ends of dreams and a grey stream
  of crocodile tears curling between bones
  —the remains of other beaten keepers,
  who have failed even at this, the last act of retrieval.
  You are alone, deep in the noxious silence,
  but now you must turn, you must turn
  and try to make your way back.
- Always bring a hat.

Hill-Climb Time Trial

My bike is a lie detector.
It grades them all from white to black.
To lose weight I ditch a reflector,
and yet my measure still comes back.

What you gain is what you lack,
bent against the hill's steep proof.
You cross your heart at each switchback:
two wheels and the truth.

2 Accounts

The day the bottom fell out the housing market,
I sussed my landlord about the fridge.
'It wanders,' I said. 'When I get up
it's in the middle of the kitchen. Once
I got home and it was like halfway down the hall,
straining at the plug.' 'Huh,' said the landlord
and wedged StopGap under its feet.

The next day I came home and it had like
totally scarpered.
There was only a dust-grossed square
and this old piece of cash from the visionary 2020s.
I pocketed the cash and sussed the landlord.
'Tell it to the bank,' he said
and rang off.

By the weekend the flat was a tell-all of dust squares.
The landlord moved in.
He was a nice bloke (he said), which (he said)
was part of his issues.
I sucked it up, worked online, ate fluff.
The landlord was a random cook.
I blinged him at Hiphopoly.

As it turned out, the bank sussed it to me first.
The numbers didn't stack up.
It was Sunday, my day to go outside.
'Lend him time,' I said. 'His back is carked.'
'Time is money,' said the voice.
'No,' I said. 'Time is turtles
—all the way down.'

One day I came home and the fridge was back.
The landlord was inside it.
I sussed the bank.
'Is this like some metaphor?' I said.
'Money,' said the voice, 'is the only metaphor

worth discussing.'
There was a caution-pause and,

in the chill rented light, I suddenly saw
where we were at, which was
the end of meta-narratives of value.
After mega-years buffing it out, it seemed all
—minusing one—were now subsided.
'His assets are naturally frozen,'
said the voice. 'Your move.'

Games are the negatives of beauty, truth
and sleep, but such clamours were now over.
So I converted. I sussed an account.
I divested and invested.
The numbers flicked and flowed
and I flicked and flowed with them.
Fractions speak louder than words.

So like here I am, via you scrolling
me over. I look good on paper.
Only sometimes, when the fridge pours me
a long cool one, do my evenings turn turtle.
Pang, our hearts once said, when stretched to bursting.
For now our figures remain buoyant.
Invisible hands gather us in.

Avoiding Janet Frame

My friend Ben Wilde
from Palmerston North
came flying
out his driveway out

of control on
rollerblades and
just about
'cleaned her out'

the 'poor old thing'
as she
toddled along Dahlia Street's
fraught suburban footpath.

'Imagine if I'd killed her,'
he said.
'That would have been
a turn-up for the books.'

Anna's Nightmare Solution

The Minpins gave me nightmares.
I was Little Billy being chased by the Spitler.
So I changed it so I was the Spitler.
And I ate Little Billy.

Popocatepetl

We joined the lines of truth and prattle,
sense and nonsense, Hansel, Gretel,
rhyme and rhythm, hand and rattle
—and up popped Popocatepetl.

So we headed for the chapel.
All of us were in fine fettle.
All were chancing tittle-tattle
on brittle Popocatepetl.

Pansies, daisies, bluebells, wattles;
fingers stung by stinging nettles;
peaches, pears and plums in bottles
—ill got on Popocatepetl.

Farmers lopping sheep and cattle
—skinned knees daubed with purple Dettol—
prime cuts primed for prime-beef battle
chucked off of Popocatepetl.

Pop said it's our choicest chattel.
Ma said pop it in the kettle,
or that unstopped glottal scat'll
unsettle Popocatepetl.

Voices rose to heed the steeple;
volcanic trickles leaked red petals;
discombobulated people
flop flipped on Popocatepetl.

Threads were starting to unravel
(the LSO played heavy metal);
Flat Earth folk not on the level
belittled Popocatepetl.

The peak was running out of petrol.
The setting sun refused to settle.
The crying of a dying petrel
swung low o'er Popocatepetl.

Lost causes without a rebel;
rising hackles, pocked collateral;
the bass clef might become the treble
and topple Popocatepetl.

If you google, then the web'll
throw up fatal endings et al.
Go now bubble, bird or pebble
—be free of Popocatepetl.

The BBC Sessions by Belle and Sebastian

Listening to Belle and Sebastian wind into their song
'Me and the Major' live in Belfast, 2001,
I think how it would be the ideal time for them to
alter the line 'he remembers Roxy Music in '72'
to 'he remembers Stiff Little Fingers . . .' even

though it would lose its rhyme and scansion.
'He remembers all the punks and the hippies too,
and he remembers Stiff Little Fingers in '78' sings Stu
-art Murdoch—with whom I'm immediately in love.
Later in the concert, the band (which I now consider myself part of)

invite an audience volunteer—Barry—on stage to sing.
He suggests The Velvet Underground's 'I'm Waiting
for the Man', which the band charge into pell-mell
almost before he's finished speaking. Yet he sets himself
and sings it through completely—without hesitation, deviation or

indiscretion. He's no singer, but somehow it soars.
Rock and roll, I love it. You get through
your fifteen minutes in three, and who
cares if you sound like a wet cat
being dragged down a blackboard toward a vet.

So when you purchase Belle and Sebastian's *The BBC Sessions*,
make sure you get the deluxe edition
with the bonus live CD.
Not for me,
for Barry.

Beyond Words

As a child, a flatmate of mine had a recurring nightmare in which she was pursued by yellow dots. The dots, which were sometimes big, sometimes small, would chase her until she burst awake terrified just before they caught her. Her concerned parents took her to a psychologist who, after careful analysis, concluded that the dots represented 'non-specific anxieties'. Which is why I've always kept the following to myself.

In my recurring childhood dream I was a swan. The dream always left me distressed, although all it consisted of was me swimming around and around my pond honking. I would reach a state of intense agitation, but I've no idea what over. There was no one else in the dream, though I always felt I was trying to communicate with someone. The circuits of anxious, illiterate honking would build until I woke to the obvious pun that the dream was my swan song. Puns are typically the last refuge of middle-aged males, which makes my childhood look even more embarrassing. I never did work out what I was trying to say. Goodbye, I guess.

Willie's First English Book

Mahi 1

In that house. In the boat. In the ship. In this basket. Tell Mary to come in, it is cold. A little girl fell into the river, and James ran in after her. The dogs are in our house. There were many ducks in the river this morning. Where is the gun you had in your hand? The boat is in the river. Did you read that in your new book? We went there in the name of the Queen. The little pigs are in the mud. Are my new pens in your box? No, they are not in my box, they are in John's big box. Where are our boys? They are in the house with Paul. I saw our old red cow in the wood. Is my hat in its box? No, it is in my house, on my box.

Mahi 2

Much good is said of this man. They speak evil of that man. Their garments are made of wool, ours are made of flax. We like flax garments. John is the brother of James. Mary is the sister of James. The men of that place were not in the boat. It is wrong of them to speak evil of us. There, in that tree, is the nest of a parrot. That is the red bark of this tree. There is the house of Paul. That is the food of our pig. Here are the two lost horses of John and William. Their little girl died of a fever this morning. The dogs of the five men we saw yesterday killed two of our pigs. What do the men say of Thomas? A basket of apples.

Mahi 3

Go to Mary. Take this bird to her. Give the gun to James. Bring the fish to the house. Our two boys went to the wood to their brothers. Their three dogs ran to bite our little pig. I gave some sugar to him. Mary gave some sugar to the boys. They gave some of their sugar to us. What do they say to us? What did Paul say to me? To whom will they give their gun? Will they give it to John? To whom didst thou speak? Strive to read well. Carry the basket of eggs to the house to Mary. We did not speak to them, we spoke to Paul. Tie these three ducks together, and give them to Ann. As 2 is to 4, so is 4 to 8. I can count to 100 (a hundred), and John can count to 1000 (a thousand). Pay me the money that is due to me for my work. Tell me what money is due to you for your pig.

Mahi 4

A boy is on the house. Our hens are on that tree. We were on the wharf this morning. On our way to the sea we saw our lost cow. That cat is on John's back. On each side of the black pig were two dogs barking at him. On seeing us, Paul said, come in and have some food. In this month, on the sixth day, they were all here with us. The sun shines on the tops of the tall trees. It rains there on the sea. It rains on the high hills. Tell John to put our saddles on our horses. On hearing Paul, we said, on whom do they put the fault? Paul said, they put the fault on Thomas and on James. If you come on that day we shall all be here. Mary and Jane will go to town on that day. There is mud on their books, and on your gun.

Mahi 5

They caught four good pigs with their three dogs. I killed four birds with the gun John gave me. The men are going to the ship, may John go with them? Jane cut her hand with Paul's big knife. With whom of these girls is the truth? Is the truth with Jane or with Mary? John cut down a totara tree with Paul's big axe. James caught the owl with his hands. The three good boys are going with John to-morrow in the new boat. We cannot go with you to-day. Their pigs must not stay here with ours. Our new boat sailed well with the wind. Their dogs are not going with yours to the wood. Those boys must not go with us.

Mahi 6

Men say, there are good things in this place. Thomas reads often in his new book. I saw a very large peach tree in Paul's garden. There was no fat in the ox we killed. We saw the gun this morning in this place. You saw our red cow in the dell. Why do you walk in the rain? We went on the sea in John's new boat. We cannot see in the dark; an owl can see in the dark. We walked to John's house in the rain. We saw the pen in your hand. Is it in that box? No, it is not in that box. The girls' new books are all in this box; we saw Mary put them in yesterday. The cows are come into the garden. It is night, shall we go in? You can go in, I shall sit here in the door, to see the stars.

Needs Work

You decide to start again. This time, you listen to your parents.
No, you don't. You walk into the forest.
This way. Between these trees.
You like to watch people unobserved.
You like to think about nothing. The space it requires.
The time. You drift along the lines.
When you read, whose voice do you hear?
That sadness you sometimes feel. There? Not there?
Have you ever held on too long? Hold on.
What was your grandmother's maiden name?
You'll have to go back. Between those trees.
You'll have to go on. A reassuring sign.
Here come the margins. Softly. Firmly.
Percentage. Leakage. A nice little earner.
The customary world. According to custom.
People in space and time. The illusion of choice.
The tyranny of choice. Partial information.
Uncertainty. A strain of influences.
Decisions based on networks, hunches, haunches.
Emotions made flesh. Shuddering details.
Good feelings. Bad ideas.
Everything is manipulative.
Soft crotchets. Silence. Actual size.
And always the Big Generals.
Mr Unknown. Mrs Unknowable.
Ms Impossible Spirit. Miss Understanding.
You like a good joke. Does that count?
What about Stan and the Cellphone?
The curve ball? The double curve ball?
Questions. Answers.
Sometimes the answers just come down the phone.
Forget love. You cannot replace it.
Follow love. It will consume your life.
Accept your lot. Don't accept your lot.
Don't join the army. Don't romanticise manual work.
Get a grip. Regain the initiative.
You regain the initiative. But lose focus.

Broad brushstrokes. Depth of field. Negative space.
Nothing you can put your finger on.
You keep on. You could never let things go.
Love's metaphors. Metaphor's warm auditorium.
You slip in at the back. You like to watch people unobserved.
The unwritten rules. Indoor/outdoor flow.
Tongue and groove. Tongue in cheek.
A rustic little charmer. Your own patch of paradise.
Needs work. Needs new shoes. New friends.
Both oars in the water. Haha hoho.
Needs to let go. Start over.
Fresh ideas. A breath of fresh air.
No more apologies. No more nos.
Sorry. You're fresh out of luck.
Missed boats. Loose cannons. The hospital tuck.
Ships that pass in the night.
Darkness. Light.
A flock of seagulls. A flight of steps.
Streamed consciousness. Abandoned sex.
The edge of a crossing. Stillness.
Fullness. Imagination's flossing.
The unlevel spirit. Bless it. Blast it.
Groups and their creations.
Gods. Religions.
Abstractions. Equations.
Particles and waves. Both right and wrong.
An hesitation. Don't worry.
You're the sharpest knife in the poem.
You keep it together. You stay on song.
Cadences. Occasional weather.
Things so much depends upon.
Thought bubbles. A red umbrella. Smiling.
Passing by woods on a snowy evening.
Desire's clarity. A clearing.
Hairs on tan lines. Lines in the sand.
Boundaries as possibilities. A study.
Listen to your heart. Listen to your body.
Baby steps. Sibilance. Minor dings.
The inevitable compromise.

Time flies. Time drags. Time slips.
Time sings.
And then it is time.
Windows. Curtains.

from *Floods Another Chamber*

Opening

There is too much
poetry in the world

and yet

here you are.

Flying Fuck

We spend too much time
doing things for people who don't
give a flying fuck about us.

What is a flying fuck anyway?
Is that line earning its place?
It could probably be cut.

A Light Copy-edit

Some people are
sharing a joke, passing it back and forth,
adding bits on until it is just
hilarious. OMG. I guess you had to be there.

You run your thumb across the tips
of your fingernails. You touch your tongue
to your lips. Outside, a vapour trail
crawls across your eye.

Your screen talks to you.
Hi, it says. Can you please do this?
How long do you think it will it take you?
How long?

Gloss

I paint the surface of the slick machine.
Day 1: Brushed away the cobwebs, tossed the crutch.
It's vital to first scrub the surface clean

before going through the undercoat routine.
Day 2: Really should have moved the couch.
I paint the surface of the slick machine

to get ahead, not back to where I've been.
Day 3: Forehead clammy to the touch.
It's vital to first scrub the surface: clean

until it's focused, singular and lean.
Day 4: Some rocking, mouth a slouch.
I paint the surface of the slick machine

blue for truth suffused with camo green.
Day 5: Crying uncontrollably and such.
It's vital to first scrub the surface clean

and polish any vowel sounds to a sheen.
Day 6: Blank, no leakage, nothing much.
I paint the surface of the slick machine.
It's vital to first scrub the surface clean.

Social Experiment

While the 2011 Rugby World Cup final was live on television,
I went for a bike ride round the Miramar Peninsula.
I was interested to see how quiet it would be and who else,
if anyone, might be about. A car turned a corner in the distance
and I wished I could reach out to it and interview
the occupant.

I was in the airport vicinity, so also saw
a couple of taxis, driven by, I imagined, immigrants
unmoved by our national sport and keen to work
—two incompatible traits in the
New Zealand genome.

On the lonely stretches
where there is just road and sea
—no one.
My wheels lapped the darkness.
O poetry.

In the suburbs again, there were a few pairs
of middle-aged women
walking briskly.

On the empty seafront, a small gathering of youths
—the kind who hate sport and form bands.
They looked drunk or bored and I sensed
the swivelling of slow malevolent cogs
as I passed.

By now it was probably halftime.
A hush had settled over the suburbs.
Some windows framed figures huddled
round their sets like primitives
trying to keep a flame alive.
In one property, a large, second-storey window
held a solitary man staring out to sea.
Could I, after all, forgive
the country?

Emu

After a blast down Serendipity,
you begin your work in Holloway Road.
Clinical's wet trees bend their fingers over your head
like 'Here is the church . . .' Doors open
and close, but where are the people?
Highbury Fling is fast and gloamy
before a brief openness to the Sanctuary
fenceline. The wind bends through pines.
Then Car Parts. You love this section
—everything broken. On a sunny day
in the morning when the east light
falls through the trees, it's like being underwater.
Today, you *are* underwater—a tadpole
beneath the whump whump of the turbine
until you hit the extension.
The narrow sections dare you to grow legs
—so you do. Nothing like kicking a few
trees. Emu's climb starts smooth: you lock out
your suspension. The foliage falls
away and you're in barrels of grey
cloud, but the wind has your back.
Sheesh, this is the *lee* side. Round a ridge
and you scythe the jumped-up rocks
on the downhill sections like
you don't care. Nobody cares.
Just join the club. But you can't. Somehow
you pop out, churning, in one piece
and decide to push to the sealed road.
Shit. The wind really is screaming.
You hadn't noticed, what with your
relentless head, its torch song on
high rotate. Only a mad person
would make for the trig today.
What the hell are you doing?
There are no stupid questions,
only stupid answers.
Stupid, stupid, stupid, stupid.
Shallows, hollows, grey bellows.

Ghosting

A pale day, lightning
when you walk among it.

Sometimes I give in
and try to find you.

I trace and retrace my steps.
But you are nowhere.

'Go away,' I tell you.
It's one scene

after another, one
sheet of paper after

another, one
point after another

point. Then
I am beside myself.

You are beside me
then.

Peculiar Julia

Julia waltzing her name in frost.
Julia asleep on warm compost.

Julia swimming in her clothes.
Julia counting on her toes.

Julia on hands and knees.
Julia in a lettuce frenzy.

Julia swapping her Easter egg for
a Warehouse chocolate Santa Claus.

Julia stopping by the woods.
Julia reading her story backwards.

Julia perching in a tree.
Julia crying 'Can't catch me.'

Julia, wait on, hold still,
we will, we will, we will, we will.

Shrinking Violet

Violet's story started tall.
Her purple hair impressed us all.

But then her plumage went awry
and she became extremely shy.

She seemed to have no energy
despite becoming gluten-free.

Her confidence was infiltrated.
Her thoughts, she thought, were overrated.

She stopped wanting to have her say;
folded herself in half each day.

Until she was just two wide eyes
—her mouth a shrug, her shrug a sigh.

She slid like droplets down a drain.
The grim night cowls collapsed with rain.

The AM Sound

Your life is a succession of dead-end jobs.
You deliver stuff, stand aimlessly behind counters,
or stare at people's soggy sentences
until your eyes water trying to fix the leaks.
You will never be employed in an industry that makes money,
though your second 'proper' job is in a pay department.
On your first day, you are shown to your desk
in a room with other such desks lined up separately
from each other like a museum schoolhouse.
Your job is to add up columns of numbers
on a desktop calculator that prints them out
on a small roll of paper.
Each column must be added up twice
with the same answer recorded both times.
You can never get the same answer.
Your first day is an exercise in defying
the laws of maths and probability by
achieving innumerable different totals.
You start to stare at the nearest window.
Your new colleagues barely speak, but hum along to
a radio tuned to the local AM station.
'Dancing in the Dark' is on high rotate, and every time
Bruce Springsteen's yearning fills the room
the women hum and sway as they add their columns
and staple the matching pairs together.
With every repeat of the desperate riff and chorus,
your despair floods another chamber.
Bruce has his finger on the pulse of a particular strain
of suburban sadness—an aching dissatisfaction that sings
like wind through telephone wires and is
even more present when the wires are underground.
You hear its unrequited note in 'Baker Street',
the Piña Colada song, 'Hotel California' and
'I Still Haven't Found What I'm Looking For'.
You marvel at the way the sound's comforting
predictability quickly becomes the horrifyingly
inevitable so that its limitations perfectly reflect

its fans' entrapment within their own lives.
You know you're telling not showing here, but
that's kind of what's wrong with Bruce's song.
It is possible to show too loudly.
On your fourth morning, you quit.
For the next 30 years you assemble a music collection
encompassing every genre outside the AM songbook.
But the AM sound runs deep and, entering
the midmost of your youth, you catch yourself
humming Bruce's overcooked refrain as you
stare out the window at the all-too-familiar view:
a weekend DVD or dinner party, and the prep
you need to do before you paint the spare room.

Green Light

In the deep south, the winter light is clear as beauty.
There are no half measures—it stares you in the face
until you look away. But there is also imperfection.
I must insist on imperfection. I stand before the mirror
freshly bathed, my fearful lack of symmetry
half defying gravity. Full moon and waning crescent:
a smile is a scar, a scar a crescent smile.
Evening mist and wood smoke sharpen
their wispy fingers. The air is crystallising.
In Bluff, you can buy a house for $35,000.
Rotten teeth wax into a waning southerly.
There is news of an earthquake in Wellington.
More northern lies. They take our power
and now they want our resilient spirit.
Do we really need more finely turned description
to help us admire the beauty of their imagination?
Should I describe my sex life, the pearl in my oyster?
The witching hour approacheth. As a child,
I customised my Barbie to accommodate her beauty.
I stare at the sky. Perhaps the southern lights,
which I have never seen, will turn green with envy
as we roil like ferrets in the frost.
Karen, who's lived here all her life,
has never heard of them, but Edna claims
she saw them last Monday from Oreti Beach.
What was she doing out there in the dead of night?
She smiles her gap-toothed smile.
It's hard to know what to believe.
The moon, where I doubt anyone has ever set foot,
comes up and bathes my eyes
with her lowing milky lamp.

How I Met My Wife

She was standing next to her VW beetle at Piha.
'Excuse me,' she said, 'my car won't start.
Do you know anything about cars?'
I knew nothing about cars, but she was a
German backpacker who might've passed
as beautiful if you chose your words carefully.
'A bit,' I said.
She turned the key. Nothing.
'Could be . . . the engine,' I mused,
and went to the front and popped the bonnet.
What the f__!—it was empty! 'There's the problem,'
I said, 'someone's stolen your engine!' She laughed
and walked round the back and opened the boot.
Would you believe it, there was a spare engine
in the boot! 'You Germans think of everything,'
I said admiringly. 'I'm from Iceland,' she said.
I hopped in the front seat and turned the key.
The car fired immediately. I revved it a few times,
in a manly fashion, and was about to turn it off
when something told me that could be a bad thing.
'Better leave it running,' I said. 'Drive to
the nearest garage.' She smiled.
'Thank you . . . ?' 'Murray,' I said.
'Thank you Murray. I'm Eyja.'
She smiled again. 'Where is the nearest garage?
Can you show me, Murray?'
I didn't have a clue, but I got in.

White Hart Lane

That Katherine Mansfield liked
'the Tottenham-Hotspurs' makes perfect sense.
She was, after all, a modern, progressive girl
much interested in tactical intricacies.
On the terraces, her small body pushes into mine.
We share a sharp intake of breath
as the ball skitters over the crossbar.
Spurs' defenders, she tells me, are quick,
but not always able to foresee developing attacks,
making them vulnerable to salvos from the diagonal.
Her hair is damp with rain and she is shivering,
but at the next exquisite Spurs' exchange
she turns and kisses my cheek, her lips
deadly beneath the fizzing floodlights.

The Hibiscus Route

The natterjacks creaked
all the livelong night. Dawn
—black to purple to yellow—
was the compressed lifespan

of a bruise. We picked our way along
the sand, took the river route
inland. You slipped on your bum.
The flecks of gold in your eyes

glowed slightly mad, were
maddening, drove me crazy.
You returned from 'the bathroom'
swinging the folding shovel,

pointed me away so you could
bathe beneath the waterfall.
Over 50 species of hibiscus blared
their colouring competition.

You preferred felt tips, I
the softness of coloured pencils.
The awkward crayoned entries faded,
like our home lives, into the background.

We identified three new species:
lividus, purpureus, fulvous.
Back home, our partners tossed
and turned, lay fallow.

Your bruise was somewhere
between purple and yellow. Then
the funding dried up and that
was the end of the project.

Sad Dads

The sad dads are sad
because they have inherited
the Earth. Amen.

Beds R Us

Our problem wasn't roll-together
—more the opposite. Our old one was old.
We were old. Our backs hurt. Insomnia.
We worked hard. Sides to middle.
It was time to splurge. *Your* snoring.
Your leg spasms. It takes one to know one.
It takes two to tango. Loose springs. Broken nights.
3am. There wasn't enough real estate.
4am. You've got to follow your dreams.
Stains. You spend a third of your life sleeping.
It was a bargain. It was for a limited time.
The kids were jumping up and down on it.
We needed to wake up our ideas. Be bold.
These are the bedtime stories that we told.

Erotic Snowdome

The water's glitter is awkwardly real.
We lie beneath the plastic island's single palm tree
ready to copulate heedlessly, except that
everything is swimming in golden dandruff.

It speckles nipples, napes and crevices, turning
kissing into a tongueful of tealeaves.
My penis glistens with veins of fool's gold
and I worry about the glints under my foreskin,

which remind me, unhelpfully, of once standing
at a urinal and some dickhead saying
'You flashy Jewish buggers wouldn't give up, eh?'
Your vagina has never looked so disco,

but you too worry about the inside flecks
and recount, unhelpfully, the story of a woman
who gave herself a quick flannel wipe
before going for a smear test.

She was puzzled when the doctor said
'You needn't have gone to so much trouble,'
before discovering, later, that her kids
had used the flannel to mop up glitter.

By this stage we're sitting apart
blinking sparkles from our eyes
like an old Midas couple, our twinkling
assets brilliantly untouchable.

Mercy

It is so quiet in the room,
which is why you are talking.
If writing is talking.
Are words still sounds
when you read them in your head?
'Feather' brushes with its
soft consonants, but
not everyone's ticklish.
Maybe you can move a feather
up her calf muscle
until she gives a little moo.
Happiness is not a thing
in itself, it's a by-product.
The world is so fragmented.
Even your emotions lead
their own lives. These days
you rarely manage dinner together.
When you do, your emotions
grin madly while masking
well, you should know,
they're your emotions.
Neither of you is in control.
They want you to
lean in and
kiss her
edible mouth.
It would be so
easy. Impossible.
Oh, the power of circumstance.
Oh, its mercy.

Tautology Explained

Not the best poem you've
ever read, but not the worst
I've ever written.

Words

You are not going to die today
after all. Words are such blunt instruments.
You talk them round, they slip away.

They never go near what you want to say.
No, that's not what you meant.
You are not going to die today.

They pull you into their display.
Their word for you is malcontent.
They talk you round, then slip away.

'I have nothing to say
and I am saying it . . .' You like John Cage's comment.
You are not going to die today.

'Is any among you afflicted? Let him pray.'
You have the right to remain silent.
The talk goes round, then slips away.

You take your hands off the keys
and raise them high, defiant.
You are not going to die today.
They talk you round. You slip away.

Agile Workshop

I'm certified in agile • Chatham House rules • in terms of • and
yes • waterfall technique • going forward • collaborate mechanism
• create solutions • design thinking • Scrum – Jeff Sutherland •
and yes • iterative process • front end • creative end • backbone of
what we've leveraged off • align with your expectations • process
manual • starts at the very beginning • empowered with power-
points • and yes • excellent question, Lynley • noitacude • are
you across that? • informed decision • ideas • the story of the
idea • opening up the idea channels • and yes • idea generation
• external ideas • unfiltered ideas • front end ideas • high ideas
• driven ideas • tens of thousands of ideas • and yes • steal ideas
where we can • part of the ideation process • and yes • fast and
furious at the front end • decision gates • lists and spreadsheets •
templates to manage it • not wanting to put a box around it in any
way • version going online • go onto it at the backend • awkward
by design • you talk to it, Rob • and yes • stood out in my mind •
rich experience • the beating heart of design thinking • divergent
and convergent thinking • output at the backend • constraints
choke the idea • and yes • diversity • operational constraints that
exist in reality • elements of prototyping • big bang gets reduced
down • expensive and elaborate • talk to this picture • and yes •
what could that be? • think about it holistically • detailed areas of
specialty • pitch something • triaging • PRINCE2 methodology
• survive contact with reality • and yes • turn your creativity
turbo on • who is Tim Brown? • wish me luck here, folks • Steve
Johnson • chance favours the connected mind • think outside
the box • and yes • the enemy of creativity • fear of failure •
coaxability • does this align with that? • ideation • brainstorming
• just knock something out we can all see • IDEO • bravery •
empower yourself • manage large groups of people • and yes •
I wouldn't decouple yourself • we want to see lots of mistakes
• fail fast • edgy • these are choice • quick and fast decisions •
let's be real • and yes • idea decision gate • sound out • a peek
into Peter's workshop • hot segments • it's not rocket science •
social fun seekers are a cold segment • something we want to get
more in the museum of • add our voice to that • and yes • badly

taxidermied cow • put time pressures • collaborative • under the pump time-wise • touch on it • super angel • get Michael out of the tent now • hit the whole thing • in terms of the experience • engaging with the space • passive experience • out the back of that • and yes • understanding the process • the wonder of co-creation • flow diagrams • we've had to wing quite a lot of it • you're landing on your final deliverables

Ken, Barbie, and Me

We wake to the house shaking. No,
it isn't Ken and Jell-O Fun Barbie, it's
an earthquake. To celebrate, Workin' Out Barbie,
Ken, and I go outside and bounce
on the trampoline. I double bounce Ken
into the begonia.

It rains and it rains and it rains. Houses
flood, roads flood, the garden floods.
We are cut off. I send Ken for help, while
Faraway Forest Water Sprite Barbie wisely exchanges
her *en pointe* Ballet Wishes Barbie legs for
Rainbow Lights Mermaid Barbie's tail.

The volcano I audition sets the perfect stage for
Paleontologist Barbie. In safari shorts and
dinosaur-print shirt, she chips away at the lava
engulfing Ken. Super Sauna Barbie sweat
beads Barbie Makeup Artist-ically on her serene
Civil War Nurse Barbie brow.

The sandstorm catches us unawares. But
Elizabeth Taylor in Cleopatra Barbie steps up.
We lower Ken into a Tomb of Worms
then take a Barbie Sisters Golf Cart to an oasis
where Sunsational Malibu Barbie is eager for some
Sparkle Beach Barbie Volleyball Fun.

A tsunami warning blares. We pile an extensive
range of Barbie Beach Party swimwear onto a
Barbie Star Light Adventure Flying RC Hoverboard.
The moon is magnificent. Moonlight Halloween Barbie
slips sleek as a dolphin into a pink and black
Barbie SeaWorld Trainer wetsuit.

Oh no! Wedding Day Barbie's heart is
on fire. I read Fire Fighter Barbie's Safety Tips.
I trim Totally Hair Barbie's hair, then a little more,
until she's Punk Barbie—pink bob, tattoos—
'the Barbie you'll never get to play with'.
Ken takes my hand. Barbie She Said Yes! gives me

a smouldering stare. What a scene! 'Cut!'
Right on cue, Barbie Film Director's head appears
on a plate, and the credits start rolling.

Soft Returns

The broken man. The broken skin. The broken cover. The broken cry.
The broken ice. The broken curse. The broken voice. The broken sigh.

The broken light. The broken drought. The broken fall. The broken ground.
The broken tooth. The broken jaw. The broken nose. The broken sound.

The broken friendship. The broken habit. The broken circuit. The broken branch.
The broken wrist. The broken watch. The broken catch. The broken trance.

The broken spell. The broken bulb. The broken cup. The broken plate.
The broken appointment. The broken engagement. The broken agreement. The broken date.

The broken pencil. The broken silence. The broken body. The broken dawn.
The broken window. The broken record. The broken English. The broken storm.

The broken spring. The broken safe. The broken code. The broken bone.
The broken stride. The broken cloud. The broken journey. The broken home.

The broken promise. The broken surface. The broken spirit. The broken bread.
The broken hymen. The broken open. The broken needle. The broken thread.

The broken smile. The broken circle. The broken shoe lace. The broken egg. The broken rule. The broken play. The broken arm. The broken leg.

The broken wave. The broken rope. The broken water. The broken mast. The broken hold. The broken back. The broken bond. The broken fast.

The broken bank. The broken contract. The broken deal. The broken taboo. The broken connection. The broken coupling. The broken marriage. The broken truce.

The broken sleep. The broken spoke. The broken cycle. The broken chain. The broken seal. The broken nail. The broken signal. The broken rain.

The broken lock. The broken horse. The broken barrier. The broken start. The broken word. The broken vase. The broken necklace. The broken heart.

The broken line. The broken peace. The broken pieces. The broken glass. The broken chalk. The broken dream. The broken run. The broken clasp.

The broken up. The broken down. The broken in. The broken in two. The broken off. The broken out. The broken even. The broken through.

Demarcations

1. *The Violinist in Spring*

It is not the blue notes, but the blue touch paper.
It is not the short fuse, but the long memory.
It is not the small bunch of forget-me-nots, but the bed of red hot
      pokers.
It is not the brand recognition, but the subconscious associations.
It is not the warm feelings, but the doubtful sounds.
It is not the diminished seventh, but the opening chord to 'Hard Day's
      Night'.
It is not what it has been, but what it will become.
It is not the leap of faith, but the wired landing.
It is not the abandoned airstrip, but the opencast mine.
It is not the tailings, but the percentages.
It is not the dance in the figures, but the figures in the dance.
It is not the twist, but the sacrificial rites.
It is not the heart in the mouth, but the fork in the tongue.
It is not between the lines, but between you and me.

2. *Summer Near the Arctic Circle*

It is not the distance between us, but the lack of distance between us.
It is not the bonds, but the restraints.
It is not the cucumber sandwiches, but the people passing round the
      cucumber sandwiches.
It is not the cut of the jib, but the angle of entry.
It is not the long division, but the brief comings together.
It is not the bare buttocks, but the bared buttocks.
It is not the offensive line, but the defensive line.
It is not the trench system, but the high water table.
It is not the insufficient fall, but the blocking high.
It is not the big picture, but the tiny ruins.
It is not the clues, but the puzzle.
It is not the correct answer, but the pencilled working.
It is not the sound reasoning, but the popular theory.
It is not the man in the moon, but the woman in the well.

3. *Autumn Testament*

It is not the farther to go, but the father to be.
It is not the longing, but the belonging.
It is not the clasp on the purse, but the purse on the lips.
It is not above suspicion, but under the pump.
It is not the unsettled stomach, but the unsettled mind.
It is not the need for god, but the desire for god.
It is not evidence of a divine creator, but evidence against a divine
    creator.
It is not the Gaza Strip, but Gazza whipping his shirt off.
It is not talking with your feet, but footing it with your mouth.
It is not the parting shot, but the passing shot.
It is not the power, but the spin.
It is not the slant, but the enchantment.
It is not the whale in the room, but the pea in the pod.
It is not under the mattress, but staring you in the face.

4. *Mrs Winter's Jump*

It is not the words that chill us, but the silence.
It is not the silence gathering on the rooftop, but the snow.
It is not the snow falling outside, but the snow falling inside.
It is not the deepening drifts, but the lengthening drifts.
It is not eternity, but the tight deadline.
It is not the lack of time, but the lack of humour.
It is not the obvious punch-line, but the unforeseen impact.
It is not the sock in the eye, but the sock in the mouth.
It is not the cheap gag, but the cost of free speech.
It is not the failure of the imagination, but the imaginative posturing.
It is not the stroking of the chin, but the stroking of the ego.
It is not the slapped back, but the turned back.
It is not the personal preference, but the casual indifference.
It is not not caring, it is caring too much.

The Passage of Water across a
Semipermeable Membrane

An unscreened wind taxes the will
causing reflux
to rise in the chest.

Walking out would be one option—
just rip the contract to confetti
before the cocked snooks' definite articles.

But wide eyes, once averted,
absorb the blessing they believe they have coming,
and you're back with the butter mountain

which, if you don't eat it,
may well be dumped and spread
across the career you once thought was yours.

A woman transitioning into a plant
talks muka and margarine between
numbers. When the band slows down

she yells for more
root beer. She plucks a coin
from behind your ear,

and it's heads you win, tails they lose—
tough titty for those old flames flickering
like eggshell applause in empty bookstores.

The down payment is restless, ready to bounce,
as you wrote in your report, though not in those exact words.
It seems you can teach an old dog new tricks.

You part the fronds plant woman has arranged for you,
creating a curious weft in the order of
disclosure—like a generation that looks back

to look forward—because
those who cannot remember the pasta
are condemned to reheat it.

A call interrupts with symbolic news: the trucks
transporting the tukutuku panels are stuck
on The Magic Roundabout in Swindon.

You and plant woman circumnavigate
the rare Earth, splitting its differences between you.
Is that your face in a cloud

or a cloud crossing your face?
A silence you can't quite settle on
settles down.

It is late spring or early summer.
Plant woman is putting down roots.
Blossoming. Budding.

The passage of water across a
semipermeable membrane.
Here come the warm jets.

Tomorrow the green grass.
People as porous bubbles floating
within other porous bubbles. Awesome.

Drawing by Tessa Hill, c.2006

Notes

17: 'Turning Brown and Torn in Two' is also the title of a Tall Dwarfs song, *Canned Music* EP, Flying Nun, 1983.

19: '12XU' is also the title of a Wire song, *Pink Flag* LP, Harvest, 1977.

22: 'I Do Not Know' borrows/adapts some lines from Jenny Holzer's series *Truisms* and *Laments*.

32: 'Cashpoint: A Pantoum' is a found poem.

38: 'The Poem that Took the Place of a Mountain' is also the title of a Wallace Stevens poem. My poem is not intended as an elegy.

51: 'Meditation 6' is a found poem, being the logic sequence of a poem by Edward Taylor (1642–1729) as discussed in the article 'Writing' by Barbara Johnson, *Critical Terms for Literary Study* (eds Lentricchia and McLaughlin, Chicago, 1990).

57: 'Redemption' borrows stanza four's couplet from 'Autobiography' by Louis MacNeice.

58: 'Deliverance' borrows one line and adapts another from 'River Journal' by Bruce Weigl.

63: 'Welfare' borrows a line from 'Sunday in Glastonbury' by Robert Bly.

70: 'Waterford II' gets much of its information from the article 'Brand Leader' by Fintan O'Toole, *Granta* 53.

72: The lines '5 o'clock shadow, 6 o'clock rock' in 'Acoustic Demos' are, I think, somebody's entire poem – unfortunately I am unable to recall whose or where I read it.

86: 'The Cost of Living' lifts 'the Old Masters' and 'sails calmly on' from 'Musée des Beaux Arts' by W.H. Auden, and 'the small drops / stream down panes of glass . . . / gathering, / as they always have, / in pools on the ground' from 'Where I Live' by Billy Collins.

92. 'The Pursuit of Happiness' features a place called Baskerville Marsh. Scholars of Sherlock Holmes will know no such location exists, the action instead unfolding on and around the equally fictional Grimpen Mire.

108: 'Engagement' takes its final line from Psalm 18:29 of the King James Bible. 'Some seeds fell by the wayside' is from Matthew 13:4.

112: 'The Radiant Fuel' takes its title from 'The Holy Pail' by Mark Levine and 'Puff adders in the bran tub' from 'Not the Furniture Game' by Simon Armitage. The final four lines borrow their syntactical structure from 'When You're Dead You Go on Television' by Bill Manhire.

152: 'The Time of Your Life' is composed entirely of recycled phrases and includes lines from Shakespeare, Gabriel García Márquez, and Thomas Gray's 'Elegy Written in a Country Churchyard'.

171: The quote in 'The Glistener' comes from Jenny Holzer's series *Truisms*.

174: 'What the Very Old Man Told Me' is loosely based on Allen Curnow. The details are entirely invented, with the exception of the inscription in his book *Enemies: Poems 1934–36*. I am grateful to Simon Garrett for sharing it with me.

178: 'My Oatmeal Granddaughter' was partly inspired by the George Saunders short story 'My Flamboyant Grandson'.

186: '2 Accounts' was commissioned by Kate De Goldi in 2007 as part of a New Zealand Post project called *Who We Will Become?*, commemorating its first twenty years as a state-owned enterprise. The brief was to imagine what New Zealand might be like in 2050. My theme was money.

190: 'Popocatepetl' was originally published with *Sport* 38 as a set of ten cards that could be read in any order, except for the first and last stanzas. They feature drawings by Anastasia Doniants.

194: 'Willie's First English Book' is a found poem. Its extracts are lifted, almost unaltered, from *Willie's First English Book: Part 2* (published 1872) by the Reverend William Colenso. My only interference, apart from presenting six of them as disjunctive prose poems, was to delete one line.

197: 'Needs Work' tries to subvert some common, and entirely sound, writing rules by using fragmented details, generalisations, abstractions and clichés to develop a narrative of a life. Each fragment links to those around it some way, be it through sense, suggestion, sound, allusion, illusion . . .

209: 'Ghosting' was written for Te Papa Tongarewa's *Walk With Me* project (2014). Poets were asked to respond to Colin McCahon's painting *Walk (Series C)*, painted in memory of his friend James K. Baxter.

216: 'White Hart Lane': Katherine Mansfield's enthusiasm for 'Tottenham-Hotspurs' is noted in *Katherine Mansfield: The Woman and the Writer* by Gillian Boddy. There would not have been floodlit games in Mansfield's day.

224: 'Agile Workshop' is made from phrases I wrote down during such a workshop in 2013.

226: All the Barbie doll types in 'Ken, Barbie, and Me' are real.

230: The section titles of 'Demarcations' are titles of poetry books by Anna Smaill, Lauris Edmond, James K. Baxter and Jenny Bornholdt.

236: Thank you for reading.

Index of Titles